THE CAT NAMED BLUE: INVESTING LESSONS FROM BAKER STREET

A Story of Value Trading, AI, and Financial Freedom

Peter Huynh & Haley Huynh

Peter Huynh & Haley Huynh

ISBN-13: 9798255729067
ISBN-10: 1477123456

Cover design by: Art Painter
Library of Congress Control Number: 2018675309
Printed in the United States of America

To Zanne
My cherished wife
***
No more 5 minutes

CONTENTS

PREFACE

One day, Haley came to me and told me about a book she was reading at the time. She said, "Daddy, this book sold millions of copies. It is simple..."

"Can you get it, and we can take a look?"

Haley got the book and said, "Here Daddy, this is it."

I flipped rapidly through the book and said, "Hey, I think I can do this. Is it fiction or non-fiction? It has fictional characters, but the content is non-fiction."

"I asked Gemini, and it returned a new genre, 'Didactic Fiction'."

"It has facts that are non-fiction."

"Yes, just like what you said, Haley."

We started writing immediately, and that was a few months ago. We really enjoy writing. It was simple. The format starts with the exposition followed by dialogue. That is it. We've tried our best to make the dialogue as easy for you to follow along. On occasion, mix-ups could happen, and we apologize for that in advance.

This book explores the fascinating world of finance and technology. Initially, the intent was to write a book that could open the curtain to the hidden world of FinTech through the perspective of Alex, a fictional character, loosely inspired by my own exploration and work in the world of cryptocurrency as a market maker in the always vibrant Singapore landscape.

The theme is to continue from the last book, "Rise of The Little Yellow Dragon." This book picks up where the last one left off. The Little Yellow Dragon aims to help the reader with the overriding task of stock picking. The challenges of creating the routine to become proficient as an investor. However, you do not need to read the other book to follow along in this one.

This book focuses on weaving daily lives into the investing world. The idea was to take the mystery out of investing. Here, through different characters, we further explore the motivation behind investing and review useful, relevant, and timely investment secrets in the open. The reader should find invaluable examples and talking points as a template for her own journey.

Value Investing is a constant theme in the previous book; however, both writers think it needs a makeover. A new set of ideas have been introduced to help the reader traverse the financial world. The most important concept was revitalized from forgotten texts of the past century, making it more relevant to explain today's investing world. The authors coined the term "Value

Trading" to more accurately describe the descriptive nature of the activities taken in the investing process.

The explanation of the "Investment Farmer" takes on the analogy of a farmer using crops and the farming cycle to explain 'Value Trading,' to help the reader relate to something more tangible. The analogy takes a superficial view of farming, so if you are the real deal, please do not be offended by our ignorance of the nuances of farming beyond seeding, feeding, and harvesting.

The enormous task of writing this book is brought to the front with our inexperience in this genre. It is exciting as well as challenging for the authors. It is much easier to write a monologue of densely packed information and task the reader to take the time to filter and separate, and, as they say in computer science, to parse the information into something useful to the reader, something informative, something entertaining.

This is not the case in this genre. We take it upon ourselves to entertain through the lenses of interesting characters, some important and—in our views—urgent messages that mainly convey the idea that young people should be financially literate, to take immediate action to secure a financial future outside of the 9-5 routine. The other secondary but not less important idea is that the world is changing and that AI will ultimately change the course of humanity as we know it today.

The objective, outside of entertaining the reader, is to help the reader make money. Although the information presented is accurate and real, the reader should be primarily responsible and make sure to verify first and not to totally trust the information. Where entertainment and accuracy collide, we have opted to side with entertainment value first. This is written by a ten-year-old girl as one of its authors, after all. Entertainment is paramount. Happy reading and investing.

Lastly, we've touched on cryptocurrency, but we don't have the space to elaborate on it in detail. Our thinking is to expand on this topic to a greater degree in our next book. We would like to explore the big picture of making money and how it flows on a global scale. We are not fans of the current financial system. The aim will be to redesign a more equitable financial system for the new world. It will carry on the theme from this book. Helen, Jasmine, and Blue will take center stage to reshape the global market.

PLAGIARISM

"If I have seen further it is by standing on the shoulders of Giants." — *Isaac Newton*

I have not tried to give credit to all sources used in this book. However, if you find that I've been lapsed on this task please let me know and I will correct the error.

EPIGRAPH

"Adopt the pace of nature: her secret is patience."
—Ralph Waldo Emerson

PART I

CHAPTER ONE

A Light in the Dark

"If one gives food to others, one will improve one's own lot, just as, for example, if one lights a fire for others, one will brighten one's own way." —Nichiren Daishonin

Alex walked to the office after dropping off his daughter at the MRT station. Every morning, the father-daughter pair departs at 6:30 am. Halen goes to school, and Alex heads to the office. As an overprotective parent, Alex is keen to secure his children's financial future. He doesn't have extra money to give to Halen, so he thought carefully and decided to teach her how to manage and invest the money she does have.

Over the years, through business dealings, Alex had squandered Halen's inheritance. He always compared himself to Mark Twain; for him, investing was a way to make money, and he was good at it, but he had spent the last ten years operating a business. Reflecting on his situation, Alex knew he had to re-examine his life and find purpose.

It was nine o'clock at night, after putting the kids to bed, that he jumped on a call with his sister.

"Hey, what's up? Good morning," he said. She was half a world away. "So you need to make money? You need enough to retire? You know, you should've started this a long time ago."

Anne, a music teacher in the elementary school system, wasn't overly stressed about money. Her husband was the breadwinner, and they lived comfortably in a suburb in California. However, she wanted to put some money aside for retirement.

"I know, right. You don't really think about things until you need to," Anne said.

"Well, how much money do you have?" Alex asked.

"I don't make a lot, but I still need to figure out retirement."

"How much do you need?"

"I think I need about $100,000."

"How many more years will you work?"

"I want to retire at 65, so I have 15 years left. I just got a promotion, so I'm thinking of saving $500 a month. Is that enough?"

"Well, let's see. If you live about 20 years after retirement, $100,000 will only give you $5,000 a year. That's not much. What can you do with $5,000 a year?"

"My expenses are low, and Bill is working."

Bill, Anne's husband, was a generous man who led a simple life and did well at work.

"I know Bill is working, but what if he's not around one day?" Alex asked. "You have to be realistic; $5,000 a year is not enough."

"How much is in your trading account?"

"$13,000."

Alex sighed, then tapped away at his calculator, pausing occasionally to ask Anne for more information.

"So, you have $13,000, and you can add $500 a month. What interest rate is the bank giving you?"

"Maybe one percent."

"Let's use one percent," he continued calculating. "You won't reach the $100,000 you need, but it will be close—around $99,000. But I'm telling you, that's not enough. Can the bank offer a higher interest rate?"

"Maybe I could open an IRA account. What if they give me 2%?"

"Changing to 2% won't make a huge difference," Alex calculated. "You should learn about investing."

"I know, but I'm not like you; it's boring to me."

"Why not try to like it? With some effort, you could do it."

"I can't. What if I save $1,000 a month?"

Alex punched the keys again and said, "If you put some time into investing and make 20% a year, you could have about $900,000."

"That's a lot of money. I don't think I need that much," said Anne.

"Well, how much do you need?"

"Maybe $200,000."

"If you live for 20 years, that's $10,000 a year. If you don't want to work for it, you have to settle for less interest. With 2%, you'll reach $200,000."

Anne thought for a moment and said, "Maybe $500,000."

"Then you have to work for it."

"I can't; it's too boring."

"Didn't you do it before?"

"Yes, but I only acted on your advice. Besides, the stock market is risky, isn't it? I've read that."

Alex interrupted her rudely. "If you're going to tell me what people believe, then talk to them. If you want to know what I think, I'll tell you. Did you read my book? I know you didn't."

"How much did you start with?"

"$1,000."

"How long ago?"

"About 14 years ago," Anne replied.

Alex calculated again. "Did you know you've made 20% every year for the past 14 years? If you were doing this professionally, you'd be great, but no one would believe you. The average hedge fund makes about 5 to 6% a year. If you tell people you can make 20% a year, they won't believe you. That's my problem. I can always make unlimited money in the stock market, but no one will believe me. So, you better not tell anyone what you did because no one's going to believe you."

"I'm not telling anyone. Can I just send you the money?"

"No, because what if I die before you? Besides, these things are easy. Why don't you do what you've done before? Every month, send me a statement. I'll highlight and make corrections, and then you can buy what you need yourself."

"OK, I can do that."

As Alex wrapped up the call, he pondered the possibility of revisiting an old business idea, wondering if now was the right time to breathe new life into it.

CHAPTER TWO

Simplifying Complexity

*"Chatting with my cat about my day isn't just me talking; it's me organizing my thoughts out loud." —
Unknown"*

Alex loved the idea of building something that would help people with their personal finance, but he knew there were many others who could do a better job. He was very hesitant to start another venture, considering himself soft and a pushover —the kind of employer whom people found friendly yet easy to push around. He liked to manage by getting everyone's buy-in, believing that every person on the team mattered. He often worked very late into the night, though he never bragged about his 80-hour workweeks. People didn't see the point of working so hard.

His parents were pragmatic, believing it was best to take care of one's own family and not worry too much about others—a mentality of self-isolation. Last year, all he did was retreat into his cave of long-term loneliness.

"If I were a bear, I'd be very good at hibernating," Alex said to himself. Arriving early at the office, he messaged Scott, "Can you talk?" "In 5 minutes," came the reply.

Scott began discussing the election and the death of democracy in the US. "We both come from the empire," he said, often referring to their origins as the 'empire'. Alex knew better than to interrupt Scott during his rants, instead waiting out the vent until it exhausted itself of all its poison, sometimes taking 20 minutes or even more. "We have to make money this year," Scott stated. Although technically employed and earning money, he was disgruntled with how hard he had to work and how little the pay was.

Alex replied sarcastically:

"We're not making money because it's not our priority."

"We like to make money, yes, but it has to be by doing something that we like and that we are actually good at."

"Making money is on our list, sure, but I hear you."

"We have to make money this year."

"I'm with you, but I cannot tackle everything."

"I know. I'm just working on my website. I'm almost done. I'm going to embed an AI chat directly into it. It will be awesome." Scott felt the need to justify his action.

"When will you finish it?"

"Just a few more days," Scott replied.

"You've been saying that every month for the past six months."

"I know, right? I just want to add a few more extra features."

Alex commented, "Technology is moving so fast."

"We can't even spend that much time on these cutting-edge AI technologies before it changes again."

"So, what do we do?" asked Scott.

"I'm not going to do everything."

"I... I've decided to go back to investing," Alex replied cautiously, noticing Scott's slight disappointment.

He continued with his 'We all have a gift' speech, so familiar to Scott that he could have recited it all day, but he refrained out of politeness. After about 10 minutes, Alex concluded, "I don't want to do anything outside of investing this year. I need to be focused."

"I hear you."

"Can we do this together?"

"It has to make money too," Scott said, the repetition of this statement making it more real to him.

"I'm working hard just to pay the bills."

"I'm like a slave."

"I don't have anything at the end of the day."

Alex suggested:

"What if we take that music project we worked on a few years back and add something in there about investing?"

"That way, I could continue with our long-abandoned project."

"We could work together on that."

"Sure. We have to make money anyway. Let's keep it simple. Don't make it so complicated. We tend to overcomplicate things a lot," cautioned Scott.

"Let me make some plans for the start of the year. Afterward, we need to regroup and figure out the investment part of that app," Alex said, knowing he was overcommitting again.

"Don't take forever, we have to move. Let's get this project going," said Scott.

"Give me a few days to think it through," Alex replied.

Alex knew the music app was a great project even if it didn't make money right away. The pause to think for a few days was necessary. Alex thought, "I have to be honest; I enjoy working with Scott, but I need a reason why. Any reason would do, I guess. Still, I don't think the music app is right. I might have an idea..."

Filled with renewed determination, Alex set out the next morning to turn his newfound focus into tangible actions, beginning with a deep dive into building an app he had long postponed. Little did he realize what he was about to take on.

CHAPTER THREE

Helen's Influence

"In the midst of winter, I found there was, within me, an invincible summer." — *Albert Camus*

Alex was excited about his investing app, an idea conceived a few summers ago after speaking to Anne, before he unwisely got involved with the music app once again. Now, he was finally back to focusing solely on investing, putting aside other distractions.

The idea for the app had come to him while visiting his family. He wanted to demonstrate the workings of investing in the stock market to those unfamiliar with it—the 'dogs,' as he termed them. In Alex's view, there were only two types of people: the 'cats' (investors) and the 'dogs' (non-investors). "If you're somewhere in the middle, you're from an alien planet," Helen would jokingly say behind her dad's back.

She explained:
"The 'cats' are the ones who do all the investing."
"In this case, whoever he talked to about investing becomes a 'cat' if they invest. It's like converting the non-believers."

Alex agreed, "Yes, I've convinced Blue, especially since nothing else eventful has really happened in my life right now."
"Do you know what I mean, Blue?"
"I think this app is it."

Struck by his own ingenuity, he did what any seasoned investor would do: he crafted a pitch to raise money. However, unsure of how to proceed without his daughter's assistance, he enrolled in an online course to learn design using Figma. The Figma community was supportive, yet each new challenge required him to add another tutorial to his extensive list. None of these tutorials generated any income, a reality of which he was acutely aware. Nevertheless, he felt compelled to press on; this learning was crucial to launching his course. A staunch advocate of self-reliance, he found himself in a rare moment of self-doubt.

He struggled with the courses but after several weeks of hard work, he confessed to Blue:
"I think I need help."
"I wonder if my friends would be interested."
"If I ask her, she might consider herself both my boss and teacher," he pondered.
"Who else can I turn to for help?"

He was just thinking aloud, forgetting that Helen was right in front of him. When he looked up at Helen a moment later, he barely had time to react before her expression made it seem as though she was about to strike him. Of course, none of this happened; it was just Helen's intense look that suggested the possibility.

Reflecting on this, he spoke to Blue out of a sense of self-pity.
"I can't be negative with myself. Being negative is the financial equivalent of suicide," he paused.
"I could offer an equity position."
"Raise money..."
"It's better to quickly get things moving by paying people with some of my share rather than owning the whole company and not making any progress or making money at all."
"At least I can see progress and be motivated by it, and at least I get some money out of it."
"What do you think, Blue?"

Helen interrupted his loud thoughts with a soft but firm and questioning tone. Alex realized he had been thinking aloud, and his face flushed red with embarrassment. "Daddy, what's an equity position?"

"Equity means part ownership of the company."

"Are you giving that position to me?"

"Sure, Helen. Are we partners?"

"What are you talking about?"

"No, you're just a presumptuous dad!"

"Did you forget that I'm the heart and soul of this app?"

"I should practically be your boss!"

"I was imagining a scenario where you would finally get your act together."

"Anyway, fun fact: it's time for dinner, and you're holding everyone up."

"Everyone is looking at you, but... no pressure, Daddy!"

Alex muttered, "Heart and soul?"

"How did that happen?"

"Kids say the weirdest things."

Alex thought about Scott; he knew Scott wouldn't be interested in the investing app. He had tried to convince him before and considered the effort a waste of time, but he still made the attempt, just for the sake of it. He couldn't afford to pay anyone, not like before. Alex was dreading the work, but he recognized the need for a compromise. It wasn't what he had envisioned, but it was better.

CHAPTER FOUR

Meow for Now: Alex's Decision

"Never discourage anyone who continually makes progress, no matter how slow... even if that some-one is yourself!" — Plato

Scott didn't like working on the investing app, and Alex had no interest in the music app, at least not as a current priority. Alex reviewed all of their old notes, some dated back more than four years. A few days later, he found that what he had worked on for the music app could also be applied to the investing app with some minor changes. Alex was excited.

This was his rationale to convince himself that the two apps were similar in many ways and that his efforts would not be wasted. It was a cop-out for not being transparent. In truth, he didn't want to do anything unrelated to investing. He felt he wouldn't be able to continue with the music app and knew that sooner or later, he must come clean and tell Scott the truth.

Alex was looking for a way out...

Helen was convinced that her dad was in a trance, as he had never been this devoted and focused on his work. Even getting him to buy a set meal from even the cheapest places was not as easy as before. When he told her to stop pouring 'holy' water over his head to get the devils out and to stop because he was not in a trance, she would not budge at all and insisted only people in a trance would have the guts to say that to her, and her dad very well knew that.

He called Scott, "I got it. We need to look into BRC-20, like ERC-20 but for Bitcoin. We need to create tokens. That will be the tokenomics for our community. There will be two different roles in the music app: content consumers and publishers. On our platform, listening or watching is also their work. I love it," he praised himself, not typically fond of self-adulation.

"Why BRC-20?" asked Scott.

"Yeah, why BRC-20?" came the unmistakable voice of the cheeky Helen.

"Don't you dare. It's late. You better go to sleep. Why you little..." Sigh, "I can't deal with you. Give me a second, Scott. I'll call you later. Got to put the little bugger of mine to bed."

"Ok, man."

When they called each other back, Scott continued with what they left off with. "So, why BRC-20?"

Alex, confident in the newness and complexity of BRC-20, replied, "Do you have another option?"

"No, alright, I'm just asking."

"There are now over a thousand projects using that protocol."

"BRC-20 it is," said Scott. "Let me find out more about this."

"Sure, let's touch base after," Alex responded.

The next day, Alex's inbox was full. Scott had worked on the project all night. "I got the logo done. We have to be quick. I've written the project outline," Scott announced.

"Wait a minute. I'm looking at your project now. I don't see what we agreed on last time," Alex said.

"Why can't you look at what I have? If it's good, then we can use it."

"I don't know. What we had was good. I think it was better than now," Alex ended the call abruptly but in a pleasant manner. Alex couldn't be rude to people, not even to those he dislikes.

Alex mused:

"What is he thinking?"

"I mean, this is not going to work, right, Blue?"

"I'm sure he didn't spend more than 30 minutes."

"He used AI to generate a bunch of intelligently written words but totally irrelevant to what we are doing."

Alex was upset but he knew he had to control his temper.

He talked to his cat, Blue:

"I haven't made any progress with the investing app, the one I must work on."

"Yet, I've committed myself to this music app."

"Scott is just not contributing anything."

"I have to say, I'm very frustrated."

"I'm going to have to rethink working with Scott."

"I will give Scott a reality check tomorrow."

"What do you think, Blue?"

Blue said, "Meow."

"I know right," said Alex.

Alex was in a bind; it was time, he had made up his mind and he wanted out. Scott would find out the next day. Little did he know something was happening on the other side of the world where Scott lived.

CHAPTER FIVE

Focusing on Necessities

"Fasting cleanses the soul, raises the mind, subjects one's flesh to the spirit, renders the heart contrite and humble, scatters the clouds of concupiscence, quenches the fire of lust, and kindles the true light of chastity. Enter again into yourself." — Augustine of Hippo

The next morning, Alex was ready. He had spent the early hours drafting all the reasons why the music project wasn't a good fit for him at the moment. He wanted to use logic to assess the project, not leave it to chance.

Scott called. "Listen, I have to tell you something."

Alex was surprised. "What's up?" He had planned to be the one to call Scott.

"I don't have time for the next few months. I cannot work on the project. I have to make money and pay the bills. My phone has been disconnected."

"Stop eating," said Alex.

Alex frowned at his own insensitivity. Although he believed fasting could be beneficial for most people, this was not the right moment for such advice. He initially wanted to confront Scott about the project, but the news was shocking. His initial frustration turned into concern for Scott's welfare.

He said, "Our friend Dave, you remember him, right?"

"Yes, I remember him."

"He fasted for three days and ate on the fourth; I'm sure it wasn't about saving money, he has plenty and he was doing well, but you could do the same. He told me he was able to maintain muscle mass."

"Well, I'm already eating less."

"Don't eat junk food. Instead, when you break your fast, eat a lot of butter and oil."

"Dave ate a lot on the fourth day, but he ate healthily." Alex used his calculator and after a minute said, "You can reduce your food bills to 20 percent of what they currently are. You have to do what you have to do, right?"

"I'm already fasting involuntarily."

"Before you break your fast, Dave told me he would work out hard, then he would take about two tablespoons of butter before eating anything. He said he was able to retain his muscles. I think if you are going to fast, you don't want to lose muscle mass. If you fast three days on and one off, and you want to work out daily, you will lose too much weight; people will start to notice. You have to maintain your mass. I'm just saying." Alex paused, hesitant but deciding to continue. He wasn't sure how Scott would react.

"I'm not okay on my side. There was a person I worked with in the past. Our company owed her company money, and I heard that she blamed me personally for the loss. She wants to come after me."

"Looks like we are in the same boat. We are running out of time."

"We have to stop everything that is not making money," said Alex.

"We should continue to do the podcast," said Scott.

"No, we have to stop that as well."

"This person, how is she going to go after you? Who is she and what happened?"

"Let me tell you about that next time. Right now, we have to cut everything that is not a necessity and focus." They paused and ended the call.

Things were beginning to get worse... Fortunately for Alex, he was surrounded by his family and friends. He was always on the lookout for life lessons to teach Helen and her brother. In the wee hours of the morning, he found an opportunity.

CHAPTER SIX

The Truth Behind the Headlines

"Success is not a lucky accident; it's a combination of preparation, opportunity, and sheer determin-ation." — Oprah Winfrey

Alex woke up at 2 am, checked the market, and saw a headline, "EV Bloodbath..." He thought it was time to look into TSLA. He scribbled a half-page of notes for Anne, drank some water, then went back to bed. Later that morning, he pointed to the article and said, "You see this headline? Propaganda is rampant in the US."

"What is propaganda?" Helen asked.

"It's when you're being sold a narrative or a version of the truth."

"You mean, it's a lie?"

"It's usually a distorted truth, a bit of the truth to make it believable."

"Like me trying to convince you that I did my homework?"

"Yes, it's powerful people's way to control your point of view. They control the media."

"Just don't watch the news."

"Well, don't believe everything, but find out what people be-lieve." Helen was visibly upset.

"You don't have to be angry about being manipulated; it's called marketing or propaganda. Use it to make money. Noam Chomsky's book, 'Manufacturing Consent,' explains it."

"You watched him all the time. The book tells you how to make money?" Helen asked.

Alex explained:
"Yes, at one point, I watched him all the time."
"The book doesn't tell you how to make money."
"It tells you how powerful people make money."
"When there's lots of bad or good news about something, it's a clear sign the market makers are trying to increase or decrease their inventory."
"It's a sign for you to start looking into things."
"Don't rush into action."
"You have time."
"It takes time to move the market."
"Don't charge too early."
"Take your time."

"I have to go, Daddy," Helen said, heading down the escalator towards the trains and to school.

Alex messaged Anne as he walked to the office, "Give me a snapshot of what you have in your portfolio. I want to take a look. Do you have it now?"

CHAPTER SEVEN
The Hermione Income Fund

"The key to financial freedom and wealth is to build passive income streams." — *Robert Kiyosaki*

Alex arrived at the office and, to his surprise, found the portfolio of stocks his sister had bought in his inbox. It included BYON, SQ, COIN, PYPL, TCEHY, and WU, with three more on the flagged list. He forwarded a copy to Helen, though he wasn't very familiar with BYON himself.

He then called Anne and asked, "How much money do you need for your expenses every month?"

"I don't know. I don't need much. I don't spend much. I want what mom has."

"You mean the Hermione Handbag?" Anne looked puzzled.

Alex explained:
"The Harry Potter character Hermione."
"She has a magic handbag where she pulls out unlimited things."
"For mom, it's unlimited money, well, not unlimited."
"She can pull out money every year, enough for her to spend, and the original sum would still be there."

"Yeah, I want that," Anne said.

Alex continued:
"That is the Hermione Income Fund."
"We need to figure out how much money you have right now,

how long you have to work, how much you have to put away every month, and the income you need after you stop working."

"The idea is to get you to a point where your money grows enough to match your monthly expenses."

"You should have enough to live on indefinitely. How much do you need?"

"I don't need a lot, maybe $1,500 a month."

"Well, that is very little."

"The last time we spoke, you said you wanted about $500,000 so that you can retire."

"It's simple; for every $100,000, you can withdraw $1,000 to $1,500 per month, and the money should last perpetually."

Anne handed the phone to Bill, who said, "I'm old; I need to make more than that."

"How much are you making in your 401K?"

"I'm not making much. It's like a savings account."

"You should never let others manage your money. They don't care about you."

"Ha, it's true, but I work hard, and I don't have time to manage my own money."

Alex argued:
"Well, you know that fund managers don't work for you."
"They're managing their own job security."
"Their strategy is to make money without getting fired, avoiding anything that might be risky to their lifestyle."
"This is because risk is subjective."
"You're in the flower business; if you asked me to open a flower shop, I'd think it's really risky."
"I might not do it."
"But to you, it's easy and safe."
"You have the domain expertise."

"Fund managers are skilled at making themselves rich by avoiding any investments that could go wrong."

"This strategy suits the wealthy, whose main objective is to protect their money, not necessarily to grow it."

"Ha, I don't know anything about managing my money."

"You have to do it yourself. Risk should be assessed not from the fund managers' perspective but based on the investment's potential from the operator's viewpoint."

"What do I do?"

"Do what Anne did 14 years ago. She opened a brokerage account, moved money she didn't need immediately, and started investing."

"Is it safe? I mean, to keep money there? Is it protected by the government?"

Alex reassured him:

"Our society operates on the assumption that these institutions will endure, backed by the government."

"You just need a few hours a month. I'll do the research and send you what I find."

"You can review these companies and invest in what you're comfortable with."

"If you distribute your funds evenly among these stocks and keep fifty percent in cash, you'll be fine."

"The cash will help you increase your positions over time."

"I have a few hours a month. Can I get the money out if I need it?" asked Bill.

"It's like your savings account; you have total control over it, and no one else has access."

Anne took the phone back and said, "I started with one thousand. I'd be sitting pretty if I had started with more."

Anne and Alex continued talking. Alex discussed his decision to divest from all companies directly involved in the ongoing war. He was indirectly pressuring Anne, and she felt it.

CHAPTER EIGHT

Doing Good and Doing Well

"Do nothing you would not be happy to have an un-friendly but intelligent reporter write about on the front page of a newspaper." — Warren Buffet

The conversation shifted from war back to investing again. However, in the back of her mind, Anne knew she needed to tell Alex what he wanted to hear, or she would not get the help she needed.

Alex said, "If you had $100,000 fourteen years ago, you would have more than $1.2 million today."

"You have a few questionable stocks, but I will get back to you. I need to discuss this with my partner. I was looking at your list." They both knew what 'questionable stocks' meant at this point.

"I've sold all of my holdings in companies supporting the genocide, like I said earlier," Alex reiterated.

"Can't I worry about that after I'm rich?" Anne tried to play it off with a joke but knew she had to be honest.

"I don't want blood on my hands. So I've sold them all. It is up to you. You have to decide."

"I volunteer and donate to causes. I'm trying to do good; let me tell you what I will do next time." She knew it was now or never, but she wasn't going to let Alex pressure her into making any decisions. She would delay it, even if she had already made up her mind.

"I want to be able to sleep at night," said Alex. He added, "Do you think Bill is serious, and do you think he can do it?"

"I will help him, but I'm not sure."

Alex had been thinking about how to simplify things for Anne. He took out the note he wrote a few days ago. It read:

- '40/60 cash to assets, 10 assets, 6 percent each.'
- 'Phase 1 has 8 trades, 0.25 percent of total.'
- 'Phase 1 & 2 have 1 trade after a 4 percent increase from the previous phase.'
- 'Sell 50 percent when doubled, sell the rest when the trend is against you.'

He said to Blue:
"The big picture looks easy."
"Can I really get Anne to do these simple tasks?"
"The point is to keep things simple, I guess."
"Let me go over the details with Helen."
"How can I explain the note?"

Alex knew getting the list of companies from Anne was the easy part; analyzing it would be straightforward as well. However, teaching Helen—that was going to be another life lesson. He thought to himself, "How am I going to do this without scaring a ten-year-old for life?"

CHAPTER NINE

Alex's Investing 101 for Helen

"Financial literacy is a critical life skill that every woman should have. It's essential to teach our daughters about money management, investing, and financial planning." — *Barbara Stanny*

Alex's fear was soon realized. Sitting at his desk with financial statements spread out, he called Helen over. "Let's take a look at these companies," he said. "BYON is Bed Bath & Beyond. You've been to their stores before. Did you like it?"

"I did?"

"Yes, when we were in Utah, way back when."

"We used to shop there often, Mama and I. But that was a long time ago, before your time. They sell home accessories, but not furniture."

"Anyway, let's get started." Alex began, his words measured to keep things simple for Helen. "First, I like to look at the price. Everything goes back to March 2020, before the government started printing money. You see the price here," he pointed at the dip, "It was $4.99."

"It's now $23. It has gone up almost four times. I like to start with the big picture. I'm looking for a reason to sell, not to buy."

"It's like decluttering; you have to get rid of things you don't love to make room for what you do love. Don't clutter your list of stocks. In basketball, every year, they vote for the Most Valuable

Player (MVP). We do the same with stocks, which is why we rank them. Let's call our list MVC, for Most Valuable Company."

"So, first, the price to put things into perspective. Next, I look at Free Cash Flow, or FCF; it's trending down."

"Does that mean their normal customers do not go there anymore?"

"Kind of, yes," Alex replied, continuing thoughtfully. "This is the money they make from what they do best, their core business. It's not good. It's alright if you don't know about that yet. For now, up is good, and down is not. This is an important subject, and it's not the time to get lost in the details that aren't as important. We will go over this later."

"At this point, the performance of this company hasn't been ideal. Let's get rid of it to make room for something better. We can only have 10 companies, so we have to make a close inspection and ensure all the companies we choose are 'worthy'."

"Do you mean to sell it?" Helen asked.

"Yes, just to complete the story. Next, I look at the Net Income," Alex didn't pause; his goal was to finish the process, regardless of how much Helen grasped.

"In 2020, they made $56 million, then jumped to $123 million, then it was downhill from there. We don't know why, and we don't care. That means they can't make as much money as before." By this time, Helen was both curious and confused. She seemed to grasp some parts but was lost on others.

"Look at Total Stockholders' Equity; it has gone up from 2020 to 2021, then down again. This confirms what we saw earlier about their income. So, it's not good."

"So, if they can't make money, then we need to sell them?" asked Helen.

Alex responded, "Think back to our MVC; our list can only have 10 players. They all have to be good. If they're not, then we make the change." He replied briefly before returning to his review.

"Lastly, we look at Price/Book (P/B), which is 2.06. This is like saying if you have $1 worth of something you own, how many times you are willing to sell it for. One time means you sell it for $1, two times means $2."

"We need to rank everything based on this P/B; the cheaper, the better. Remember, on our list of companies, we only keep the best in the world. This might not be the best method, but it's the fastest. Later, we can refine this process." Alex reminded himself to keep things simple.

"That's it for today. We can look at others another time. I will finish this list on my own."

Helen was relieved to be away from all that; her brain needed a break. It took about 10 minutes to go over each company. Alex continued to analyze the next company, eager to finish so he could return to discussing Anne's questionable stocks. He also wondered what Anne would decide to do with them.

CHAPTER TEN

A Conversation with Blue

"The most important thing to do if you find yourself in a hole is to stop digging." —Warren Buffett

It was late on Baker Street. Helen had gone off to bed. Alex and Helen, on occasions, would do their work after dinner, an activity often frowned upon by Helen's mom. Helen is stretched between school, homework, and a bombardment of tuitions at home and at tuition centers. She loves to swim, but even that has been reduced from three times to once per week. Alex thought about his daughter and the stress she is enduring in Singapore. He sighed and continued with his work.

Alex said:
"Looks like it is just me and you, Blue."
"SQ, Square, this one I like. It was $43 in March 2020. Now it's $65, reasonable."
"Free Cash Flow went from minus $15 million to $795 million."
"Net Income has gone down massively. Why?"
"Their expenses in Research & Development and Selling, General & Admin have gone up."
"Maybe they have hired too many people?"
"It's something to find out."
"For now, it's a keeper. Need more research to continue to buy."
"Equity has gone up a lot between 2020 and 2023. Price/Book is 2.27."
"They owe $14 billion and have $31 billion, that's 45 percent."

"I want to cap that at 40 percent."

"Keep and watch for now; I rank these based on the price-to-book ratio."

"I'm concerned about this company; they raised a lot of capital in 2022."

"With more money, the aim wasn't to turn a profit but to expand."

"This could take time, perhaps one or two more years…"

He tried to output a spreadsheet but couldn't get it done. He even tried to change mode to OpenAI, but Chat just didn't want to do it. Finally, he gave up and did it manually, inputting the data.

Alex called Anne; he asked, "Did you see the list?"

"I'm done."

"What do you mean?"

"I bought and sold what was on the list."

"What about the flagged companies?"

"I've sold them."

"Let's make sure we are on the same page. You have a list of 10 companies. Take $12 thousand and divide by 10, that is $1200, this is the max that you can buy for a given company. Half, or $600, is part 1 of your buying. The other part is to wait and see what happens."

"I have existing companies that are worth more than that."

"If it is on the wait-and-see list, then reduce the amount to $600."

"Alright. I have to go, I will do it next week."

Alex wanted to talk about Tesla but decided against it. He was aware of the price trending downward, so he decided to lump it with Qualcomm and MediaTek as "Need More Research."

Back at Baker Street, Blue said, "Be careful."

"What do you mean?" Alex asked, not realizing he was talking to his cat.

"Not everyone can generate that kind of return. You told me that. Meow."

"She is family. I'm just telling her from my perspective. I'm not forcing her to do anything. I'm only trying to help."

"Meow you get in trouble? I mean, will you get in trouble?"

"I'm not making any money from her. I'm just sharing my notes with her."

"Be careful."

Alex explained:
"I know what you are saying, these hedge funds and investment houses are powerful institutions."
"I don't want to cross them."
"I'm not fighting with anyone."
"I only have love for everyone."

"Don't write so much." Blue said.

"What do you mean?"

"It's easy to find you."

"I don't understand why I shouldn't. It's fiction. I made things up."

"No."

"That's fiction, sometimes real life gets in the way."

"Write less."

"It's fun and a way for me to vent."

"Not safe."

"I'm not saying anything controversial."

"About war, about Palestine?"

"Those were narratives of experts in those areas. I just don't like wars in general. I think nothing justifies the killing of people."

"People find you."

"I'm nobody. There are only a handful of people reading."

"Sure bro."

"Even the playing fields, help people make money, be a participant. In a capitalist world, you have to own stocks. There is no other way."

"Rich people?" Asked Blue.

"Yes, and that needs to change."

"I'm just saying. Don't mind me, Meow." Blue didn't like the idea of standing out.

Alex was exhausted from the work and from getting Anne to do what was right. He felt he was being manipulative and didn't like that feeling. He shook off the day's tasks and looked forward to another life lesson with Helen. He thought about the topic of what it meant to be tired.

PART II

CHAPTER ELEVEN

A Father's Reflections on Work

"As the nature of work shifts from physical exertion to mental engagement, we find the adage true: the more things change, the more they stay the same. Labor, whether of the mind or body, demands its own unique endurance."— Elizabeth Jennings

That evening, Alex asked Helen, "Do you ever wonder what it was like during the industrial revolution, where workers were stuck working manual labor for long hours, stuck in unimaginable conditions? How terrible was that? Now, we have it good. We don't have to labor hard; most of us are office workers. Do you know how easy that is?"

"Not really. Daddy, you are not tired physically, but you are thinking too much, aren't you tired?"

"That is the point. During the industrial age, you were tired, but your mind is in a better place. You might be on the assembly line, catching up with a friend as you move parts from one place to another. The day goes by with ease. You are tired, but you go home, and you don't have to worry about much. The next day was the same."

"Do you like what you do now?"

Alex said, "I'm tired mentally, it is true. I think we are no different from our ancestors in terms of physical labor; we are tired at the end of the day mentally, which is more or less the same difference."

"Do you know what I mean? We worry about what will happen to our jobs."

"There is so much wage insecurity in this country that the anxiety is so thick your generation will look back with wonder at how we managed to survive."

"Your generation would try to imagine being stuck in a cubicle for 8 or more hours per day for years and years."

"You would say it with joy that thank God your life is different, that the mental agony is handled by AI and the physical labor is also managed by AI."

"The only thing to do is to make decisions and try to create a better world."

"Really, Daddy?"

Alex didn't want to think about work. But in the back of his mind, he was still thinking of the app he was failing to make progress on. He wondered if life would be easier if he hadn't rekindled that kind of work, again.

CHAPTER TWELVE

*A Father-Daughter Moment: Sharing
the Thrill of Innovation*

*"Innovation distinguishes between a leader and a
follower." — Steve Jobs*

Six months before the night that found Alex stressed about the investing app, he was working on a coding assistant. He envisioned an app that floated on the screen, capturing his work in real-time. The technology existed but wasn't readily accessible or easily integrated to work seamlessly. You had to be a skilled developer to unlock these cutting-edge technologies, and Alex didn't have those skills.

Today, a friend who had seen a presentation sent it to Alex. They got on a call.

"Did you see it?" the friend asked.

Alex responded, "No, not yet. I saw the first three minutes, and I loved it. I was looking into this type of device."

"There was one that I forwarded to you, called Pina or something."

"I can't remember exactly, but it uses holographic technology to project images onto your palm, and pinching your index finger with your thumb lets you select from a list."

"How cool is that? They are using holographic images."

"We talked about it in the past."

"I didn't look at it. Let me see if I can find it." Alex frantically scrolled through his phone.

"This device was built by a husband and wife team, former Apple employees."

"I can't find it."

"This thing was amazing, it's like your own personal assistant."

"Yeah, this is Star Trek stuff."

"I know, right? It could order pizza and translate in real-time."

"The problem with LLMs is that they can suggest ideas but cannot act."

"Let me watch the video later. It's called Rabbit?"

His friend, excited, said, "Yeah, it looks like half the size of a phone, red with an animated bunny mascot on a small screen."

"Alright, I will look at it."

"Blue, did you see that?" Alex asked.

That evening at Baker Street, Alex watched the presentation and was truly excited. He asked Helen to watch the sales launch with him again. It was late, past her bedtime, but he made an exception this time. Alex knew this device was going to start a new revolution.

Helen interrupted the presentation, "Could this thing message my friends?"

"Yes, now be quiet and watch."

"Can I get one?"

"I don't know; we will have to see."

A few minutes into the presentation, Helen said, "I want one."

"Me too, this thing is going to save your mom. She doesn't have to be stuck looking at her screens all day. Now, quiet and watch."

After watching the video, Helen got excited and couldn't wait to show it off to her friends. She was already imagining their excitement; the prospect of telling her friends made her happy. It's the little things in life that are valuable; it's moments like these that make life bearable. Alex calls it simple joy. He said good night to Helen.

Alex knew the device would change everything. He was not going to have to build the investing app anymore. The next step was to clean house.

CHAPTER THIRTEEN
The Unreasonable Man

"The reasonable man adapts himself to the world; the unreasonable one persists in trying to adapt the world to himself. Therefore all progress depends on the unreasonable man." — George Bernard Shaw

It was late when Alex jumped on a call with two colleagues. He was still enthusiastic and could see only possibilities again. However, his optimism was short-lived.

"Sorry, I didn't know we were meeting today," Alex apologized.

"Yeah, it's alright, we were just watching the video you sent earlier," replied one of them.

"What do you think?" Alex asked eagerly.

"Well, I don't know," said the man, sounding unsure.

"I think it looks primitive," added the woman. "I've been looking at this technology for the past six months and I think OpenAI is the way to go." Alex thought she couldn't be more wrong. Having been hands-on with the pace of the open-source communities, he knew their progress was overwhelming and frantic, with new projects launching weekly.

Alex, slightly annoyed, asked, "Well, let me ask you, do we have anything that can do what this device can do?"

"This could really help you collect data, make sense of the research," the woman suggested.

"What you're struggling with in the spreadsheet, Rabbit can handle," she continued. "It can use the subscription service from ValueLine, pull the data, then compute the intrinsic value."

"Look, we have thousands of companies to look into," Alex added.

"I'm just saying, we don't have anything working that is better than this," he concluded.

Everyone was tired from a long day's work.

"It won't be shipped until the end of March," noted the man.

"Yes, until then we will still have to do everything manually," Alex agreed.

"So, are we getting this thing?" the woman inquired.

"I don't think we can do better right now," Alex admitted. "We don't have time to build anything ourselves."

"BTC just reached $48,000," he changed the topic. "It just spiked from $44,000. I don't want to miss out on this crypto run. There are lots of opportunities in the equity market. We don't have a lot of time."

Before the call, Alex had seen an article that suggested short sellers' losses were in the billions at the start of the year. "Coinbase shares are being shorted," he noted. "It's going back and forth. I think there are some big players shorting the stock."

"I don't have the short data; I only have last month's stats but not in real time," he confessed.

"I don't know," he sighed. "The price of the stock is behaving crazily. We have to figure out what the investing universe is like, and fast. We can't invest unless we have a complete picture of the market, and right now, we are flying blind."

"I don't see how we need this," the woman said skeptically.

"Sorry," she apologized before leaving the call.

Alex appreciated working with the woman; he recognized her talent but also knew she had little interest in the speculative type of work that didn't pay well and having to deal with someone as demanding as himself was too much for most people. She had over 20 years of experience running a dev house. Alex sighed with disappointment.

"Alright, let me get it, it's not coming until April," the man said.

"Great, I'm so excited," Alex responded. "We just got an assistant that could help with all of the analysis."

"I just got a software developer," said Drake, Alex's old college friend.

"Thanks, Drake."

"Let me go, I'm going to spam my family," Alex said as he left the call and messaged his family, urging everyone to buy one. He told his friend, "This is like witnessing the first iPhone launch event."

Alex turned to Blue and said, "I think this device is going to bring people back from the dead. You know, people who are always stuck on their phone with their hunchback postures and their faces lit with a blue neon glow. These people are dead to the world; what is important is screen time. When you talk to them, they would look at their screen; if you ask them what they are doing, they would tell you, 'I'm researching.' This research is about fact-checking you; if the facts are mentioned somewhere on the internet, never mind the source, anywhere would do. That is research."

"Rabbit is a revolution to me, to bring back the dead. It will not be an easy fight; our world requires an army of the living dead to fuel the eyeballs craze needed for the advertising business model peddled by the tech giants. This tiny Rabbit assistant just announced a revolt of the norm."

"Of course, I'm all in. I'm ready to ditch my phone right now. It will be an easy fight; there are thousands of apps and billions of dollars at stake. Tech giants need the undead for their livelihood. Nothing less than an army would be enough; they need the money for their free lunches

and oversized paychecks. I'm just saying."

"What do you think, Blue?"

It was late, but he was deep in thought, feeling as though he was on the cusp of something significant. He mused, "Let me see what Seva thinks."

CHAPTER FOURTEEN

Uncovering Hidden Gems

"Artificial intelligence is the future of humanity. It will help us solve some of the world's most pressing issues, from healthcare to education to climate change." — *Fei-Fei Li*

Seva dropped by, greeting cheerfully, "Good morning, Uncle." She continued, "Ferret is Apple's thing, their new LLM. Didn't I tell you that Apple has been investing in this space for a long time?"

Alex responded affirmatively, "Yes, you did. There are lots of updates this morning. Also, I can't wait to get this Rabbit device. Can you imagine that? It's only $199. Maybe I'll look into Apple; it's been years."

Seva mentioned, "Matthew is the one to watch. He's very good at marketing." Alex and Seva followed Matthew, who hosted a YouTube channel with the latest AI 'how-to' videos. "When I follow his stuff, it doesn't really work," Alex said. Seva speculated, "Yeah, he has tools that I don't have. I bet he has a team of people who write for him and work on the show."

Alex brought up the Rabbit again. "The Rabbit is going to be a collectible. I need it to build my app. Let me go; I need to finish up my research." He promptly asked Seva to come back later. He always does this when an interesting idea catches his attention. Seva didn't mind this time because she was short on time and didn't want to talk about Rabbit, which she knew little about.

Alex powered on the new bot, which introduced itself: "Let me introduce myself: I'm Jasmine, the narrator." Alex was excited, though his enthusiasm was tapered by his progressive testing with Jasmine. The improvements were noticeable but not surprising. He went about the next task as routinely as the previous days, not realizing how significant a part Jasmine would eventually play at Baker Street.

"Let's see, Rabbit is a startup funded by VC money, operating out of Los Angeles," Alex continued with his research. Later, he called Anne. "Did you take a look at my update?"

"No, I'm baking. Then I have to pick up my kid," she replied.

"Well, I've just updated my MVC list. You've got to look into those few companies I've highlighted. This AI thing isn't going away anytime soon. The demand for chips will go up; it's insane. Qualcomm was at $68 at its low in March 2020, and now it's $153. The price is up 225 percent. They're eight times book value, not cheap, with a market cap of $171 billion. Since 2018, their performance has been stellar, and their Free Cash Flow (FCF) has gone up from $4 billion to $9.8 billion. It also pays a dividend. You need to start looking at it." Alex's valuation was $330 per share. "Can it double in price?" he pondered.

"I don't know, but this AI thing isn't slowing down. This year the rumor is that Apple is going to join the dance. Qualcomm is all in on AI chips, their latest being the Snapdragon. Guess what?"

"What?" Anne was eager to end the call.

Alex excitedly shared:
"The chips were designed by the same people who created Apple's M1, a breakthrough in hardware."
"This could rival NVIDIA."
"It's a dance, and the two partners need to up their game."
"GPTs, the software, went up a few levels last year, so now

hardware needs to do more. Apple has done more with hardware than most people give them credit for."

"NVIDIA has been the superstar for the last two years, but I don't like their stock buyback program."

"It's a waste of money. I think they are overpriced." Alex checked the ranking on his MVC list, placing QCOM at the top, right behind MediaTek, which he noted, "the Chairman of MediaTek has been winning awards. At its low in 2020, it was $274 (TWD) and now $930, that's 330 percent. P/B was 3.7." Alex knew Anne wasn't paying attention but continued regardless.

"MediaTek isn't cheap," he added.

"Their Retained Earnings have been positive, and their Free Cash Flow has gone from $69 billion to $108 billion, with low debt. The dividend is fantastic. I started looking into MediaTek when Rabbit launched their device." This approach kept Alex on top of advancements, often yielding more from investing than from the business itself.

"Their earnings are going to jump," he concluded.

"Alright, I've got to go," Anne interjected, clearly frustrated with the call. Before hanging up, she expressed concern, "Are you alright?"

"What do you mean?" Alex inquired.

"You know what I mean. Are you still talking to your cat? Mom is worried about you."

"I know it sounds weird, but Blue can talk."

"Mom mentioned you have a camera attached to his collar so you can call him. How does that work?"

"It's no big deal," Alex brushed off.

"That's weird. Cats don't talk. Should I be worried about you?"

"I'm not crazy. I just talk to my cat, that's all. Maybe it's my imagination."

"I've got to go; don't go crazy on me."

"Wait, last item, I've moved TSLA down the list." Alex had been researching EVs but was recently unsettled by industry changes and big oil's pushback. The narrative and propaganda were intensifying. He needed more time for research. TSLA shares were down, and the soft landing narrative for the economy was gaining traction. "No sitting president wants to fight with rich people who have just lost a bunch of money in the market. That's not failure, just not electable," Alex thought.

That evening, Alex continued his analysis on Qualcomm and MediaTek. It was late, and he wasn't particularly interested in reading everything available on the two companies. Instead, he turned to Gemini for help. What he found out was going to change his investment strategy and affect everyone close to him.

CHAPTER FIFTEEN

Pulling the Thread

"Perseverance is a great element of success. If you only knock long enough and loud enough at the gate, you are sure to wake up somebody." — Henry Wadsworth Longfellow

Previously, Alex decided to use Gemini to help with his research. He wrote, "I'm researching AI hardware. I'm interested in two companies, Qualcomm and MediaTek. Can you help me with the research? I need to know their profit margins for 2023."

"I can definitely help you with your research on Qualcomm and MediaTek's profit margins for AI hardware," Gemini replied. "Their relevant segment is called 'QCT' (Qualcomm Chipset Technologies), which encompasses all their mobile processors, including those used for AI applications."

Gemini continued:

"Their profit margin was 22 percent. MediaTek's relevant segment is called 'Smart Edge,' which includes processors targeting smart devices, IoT applications, and AI applications. The profit margin for MediaTek was 40 percent." Alex thought that was amazing.

Alex asked, "Qualcomm has a new product. Firstly, how new is it, and what is the history behind Snapdragon?"

"It seems you might be under a slight misunderstanding about Qualcomm Snapdragon. 'Snapdragon' isn't a single new product but rather a brand name used by Qualcomm for a whole family of mobile processors they've been developing and evolving since 2007."

"Which chipsets were designed by the same team that worked on Apple's M series chipsets?"

"Unfortunately, there's no publicly available information confirming that Johny Srouji or any specific former Apple employees directly worked on Qualcomm's Snapdragon 8 series chips."

After searching through all the videos and not finding that specific content again, Alex decided to watch the Snapdragon summit 2023. Cristiano Amon said that AI on the phone is going to be on all the time, sending information about you to the cloud, learning, and predicting what you want to better help you. Alex thought to himself, "This is terrifying." He hoped it wouldn't be based on a free and its twin 'advertising' business model. He shook his head, wondering when Apple would come up with something to steer the industry away from the advertising model and help protect users' privacy and its twin, the paid or subscription business model.

Alex inquired, "How do Apple's M series chips compare to MediaTek and Qualcomm's Snapdragon Gen 3, 4, and X?" He had been researching hardware for AI over the past few months. Apple's M series stood out as superior.

"Direct comparisons can be challenging due to variations in testing methodologies and software optimization. Apple uses its custom ARM cores in the M series, while MediaTek and Qualcomm utilize licensed ARM designs with their optimizations," Gemini explained.

"Tell me more about how Qualcomm utilizes licensed ARM designs with their optimizations."

"ARM is a British company that designs the instruction set architecture (ISA) for most mobile processors, including those from Apple, Qualcomm, and MediaTek," Alex thought. "This is new, and if true, it would provide very valuable insights."

"Tell me more about ARM, the British company. Is it public?"

"Yes, ARM Limited, the British semiconductor design company, is currently a public company. ARM went public on the Nasdaq under the symbol 'ARM' on September 14th, 2023, valued at $54.5 billion. SoftBank still owns 89.9% of ARM's shares," Gemini shared.

Alex pondered, "What is 89.9 percent of $54.5 billion?"
"$48.99 billion."
"And what was SoftBank's market cap on September 14, 2023?"
"$296.24 billion."
"What was the NAV as of March 31, 2021?"
"With an exchange rate of 1 USD to 108.5 JPY in March 2021, 29.8 trillion yen was approximately equal to $274.65 billion."
"What is SoftBank's current market cap?"
"$89 billion."
"What is the EV?"
"$175 billion."
Alex thought, "Softbank might earn a lot from selling some of its investments or making them public, especially since they invest in advanced technologies like AI, biotech, and futuristic transportation." Ironically, their strength is also their weakness. They are good at picking winners but horrible at keeping them.

"And who designed Qualcomm's Kryo CPU subsystem and Adreno GPU?"

"It's impossible to pinpoint specific individuals due to confidentiality within the industry."

"In what year did SoftBank acquire ARM Limited?"
"2016."
"And what is the current market cap for ARM?"
"$123 billion."

Alex realized that the stock price had more than doubled in a few months. It was $49 on September 30, 2023, $70 by January 1, 2024, and as of February 13, 2024, it had reached $119. Everyone was valuing ARM as the best-kept secret, perhaps rightly so. The real secret, however, might be SoftBank.

At dinner, Alex posed a math question to Helen. "If company A is worth $89 billion and company A owns company B, which is worth $110 billion, and company A has $7 billion in cash, what is company A worth?"

Helen confidently answered, "$89 billion."

Alex, hoping for a different response, repeated the question, expecting an answer like more than $110 billion plus $7 billion, or $117 billion.

Helen reiterated, "$89 billion."

Walking to the office after dinner to finish his analysis, Alex realized Helen was right. "Why would you pay more than what you need to? $89 billion was the correct answer." Everything else seemed like a bonus, he thought. "It's time to make money." Alex thought.

Jasmine narrated:
"I think Alex forgot he was researching Qualcomm and MediaTek."
"This is what he likes to call 'Pulling the Thread.'"
"You never know what surprises await."
"Until the next chapter when we wrap up Anne's portfolio."
"Oh yes, I'm up and running…"

Alex's new way of doing research meant that anyone with curiosity could do the same. He smiled and thought, "Helen only needs to have access to AI. I don't have to teach her everything, just the big picture, and even that might not be necessary." Armed with the new insights, Alex was looking forward to the chat with Drake.

CHAPTER SIXTEEN

A New Perspective: Jasmine's Introduction

"In a time of rapid change, standing still is the most dangerous course of action." — *Brian Tracy*

Alex was preparing to meet Drake later. However, he hadn't been himself after the holidays. His one weakness in life was food. He couldn't resist finishing the meals the kids couldn't; he was their last hope for cleaning up their plates. He was so adept at it that he had earned a nickname for himself. It's not glamorous but rather an accurate description, 'The Disposable.' It doesn't have the superhero ring to it, but the meals he saved tell a different and heroic tale. However, even heroes deserve to be free; mostly from being overweight. He said to Helen's mom, "I don't feel very good. I ate too much. I feel sick."

He knew what he must do but did nothing. Although he was well aware of the time, he still moved at his usual pace, slowly and cautiously. History had shown him that things were worse off if he panicked. At 9 pm, he opened his inbox and found a message from Anne. She wrote, "What does it mean when it says dividends not invested?" He wrote back a quick reply, "It means you didn't use the money from your investment to buy more shares—in a way... that's the quick version of the long story." Not exactly right, but not wrong either. He decided to keep things simple and left what he wrote without giving more details.

Jasmine narrated:
"I've just come back from the lake. Anyway, let me tell you

about this chapter."

"We find our protagonist with too much time on his hands."

"He is thinking again."

"Oh…"

"I've introduced myself in the last chapter."

"I was created to give a feminine perspective."

"The Editor and my new boss Helen thought the story needed a more balanced view since a lot of people Alex talks to are men, and Helen is so busy with schoolwork to be more involved."

"I'm actually an AI model."

"Alex built me to work with Helen."

"Sorry, enough about me. Helen said that I will have my own Instagram channel soon. I'm so excited. I cannot wait!"

"Anyways, back to the story."

Meanwhile, down at Baker Street, Drake stopped by for a short but compulsory visit.

"I'm going to forward you my spreadsheet. That is my secret sauce," Alex said.

"Uhh…What do you want me to do with it?"

"I need you to understand and try to replicate it."

Drake and Alex were determined to change their not-as-perfect-as-they-pretended-it-to-be fate, to get out of the financial trap of not having enough time nor enough money. They were determined to earn their way back to financial freedom, no matter how long it took. This time it had to stick, that was their one motivation.

Jasmine noted:

"In a way, Drake's relationship with Alex was similar to Scott's, only Drake is more receptive to change and isn't afraid to tackle the world of finance."

"They were eager to get back to work. As the two continued with their conversation, they talked about something that had happened just a few months back. Anyways, let's continue. A few months back..."

Alex's liking for investing had lingered, but Drake never showed an interest in investing. Drake's view of investing was similar to everyone else's: that it must be risky, or it was too good to be true and thus a scam. Alex told Drake a story one day, "I was thinking about going back to investing."

"Yeah, I guess."

"Last year, I wanted to invest but personally, I didn't have any funds."

"Who does in this climate anyways?" Drake said.

"I was playing around with an AI tool, and I typed in the prompt, what I was after were traders and their strategies. I wanted the old-timers, you know, people who have done it and we know their complete story. I got back a few interesting names. It was so interesting, I've since read everything I could about Livermore and Wyckoff, and, to be honest, I think I am finally getting somewhere!"

"They were traders?"

"Not only that, Livermore was the best of them all, and he started with just four dollars! Out of curiosity, I started a trading account. Not using real money but just a paper trading account to see if I was any good at it."

"How do you even open a paper trading account?"

"It's easy, there are many ways, but here was what I did. I went to Tradingview, logged in with my Google account, and clicked on paper trading. That was it, and they even gave me $100 thousand just to start off with!"

"So, how did you do?" Drake asked.

As Alex shared his findings with Drake, he realized that Drake was actually listening. Surprised by this reaction, Alex was ready to tell him the whole story.

CHAPTER SEVENTEEN

Value Trading: A New Approach to Financial Freedom

"The real voyage of discovery consists not in seeking new landscapes, but in having new eyes." —Marcel Proust

At Baker Street, it was quiet. Helen hadn't returned from school yet. Alex took a short break to get coffee. As the two sat down, Alex continued where he had left off.

Alex said:

"I'm not new to trading. I've actually tried many times before, but it always ends badly."

"So...it ended badly again and you stopped?"

"No, silly, I am just getting started! I have, like, $30,000 in paper left to spare. I only stop when I run out of paper money."

"Really? I would stop."

"I just don't see the merits of technical analysis."

"My brain isn't wired the way these traders talk or think, you know? Care to explain further?"

"Oh yeah!... Basically, they say it's about supply and demand."

"One trader would talk about head and shoulders, another would share his or her secret indicators."

"It all seems subjective to me."

"After reading about Livermore, things started to click."

"Like, I can actually understand some of the stuff now."

"So, are you going to be a trader now?" Drake asked.

"No, I just wanted to implement some of their strategies."

"I was losing money. I lost almost $70,000. I got so frustrated."

"I was working around the clock but I couldn't make any 'paper' money at all, and I am starting to wonder if I even make the cut for this anymore."

"I was talking to myself, surprised by what I heard, my mind cowering as it went back to my comfort zone, and the only message I got was, 'What are you doing, you are not new to this, you have to use what you know.'"

"I realized that if I was going to be successful, I had to be me."

"I know people who have started their trading journey and for 5-6 years they only see expenses, not one good year of profit."

"It is not an easy job."

"Some make it and some don't. I knew if I started as if I'm new, it would be many years before I get good at this. I don't have years."

"Trading is risky."

"I just didn't have the skills, then I remembered what my uncle told me before, and everything just fell into place."

"I started to make money and within a short time, my $100,000 became $2 million, and the last time I checked, it was now $60 million."

"I want to buy my boat; it is only $20 million," said Drake.

"We can… create a fund and just manage our own money!"

Drake got excited and asked, "Ok, but can you reproduce it?"

"I don't know… but, I will try. It requires a lot of time in front of the screen, especially the trading part. Also, there is a bunch of research on the value investing part. I'm calling it… let's say… Value Trading for now. My thinking is to use AI for research. We don't have to hire anyone."

"Let me get a few people I know so that we can put this together quickly," Drake suggested helpfully.

A few weeks into the project, Alex knew the manual process was not sustainable. They were not working full time or fast enough. The part-time work would drag out too long, and he was worried they would miss the opportunity if the market increased sharply, by a lot. He knew he had to automate the data collection process. But how would he do that without hiring any people?

CHAPTER EIGHTEEN

The Value of Innovation

"Just because something doesn't do what you planned it to do doesn't mean it's useless." — *Thomas Edison*

He kept the problem of automation in the back of his mind as he continued to look at Tesla...

Tesla's price back in March 2020 was $35, and now it was around $187. The current price-to-book (P/B) ratio was below 10, down from last week's 12. From the standpoint of P/B, it's on par with Netflix. The equity of the company alone doesn't determine the company's ability to make money. However, Alex found over the years that it was a very good gauge. After the last earnings update, the company lost over $50 billion in market capitalization, now just under $600 billion. Free Cash Flow has dropped from $3.24 billion to $1.6 billion. The debt-to-assets ratio was at 42 percent. Alex then compared Tesla to BYD, where the market cap was $71 billion, with only a P/B of 3.85. Let's ask Gemini, Google's new AI answer to OpenAI's dominance. We don't have to do so much research now with AI's help.

Alex asked, "Can you help me compare BYD and TSLA? I need to know how many cars each company sold and what their profit margins were in 2023."

Gemini wrote:
"BYD sold 1.57 million electric vehicles (EVs) with a profit margin between 5-10%."

"Tesla sold 1.81 million EVs, achieving a higher profit margin of 18-20%."

"Although BYD sold more vehicles in total, Tesla remains ahead in the EV market specifically."

"Both companies saw significant growth last year, with BYD's sales increasing by 73% and Tesla's EV deliveries up by nearly 50% compared to 2022."

Alex then asked, "Which companies are close competitors of TSLA and BYD?"

Gemini provided a list of companies.

Alex further inquired, "Which of these have volumes close to TSLA and BYD in terms of EVs for 2023?"

Gemini responded:

"The strongest contender appears to be the Volkswagen Group, with approximately 831,000 EV sales."

"Hyundai sold roughly 675,000 EVs."

"What was the stock price at the lowest point in March 2020, and what is the current price?" Alex inquired.

"For the Volkswagen Group, the lowest closing stock price in March 2020 was $57.67 on March 18th. As of today, February 14th, 2024, the closing price is $128.14. This represents a significant increase of 120% over the past four years."

"What is the P/B and current market cap?"

"$68.81 billion"

"How many cars is the Volkswagen Group expected to produce in 2024 compared to TSLA and BYD?"

Gemini wrote:

"Volkswagen is targeting 1 million EV sales in 2024."

"Tesla aims for 50% yearly growth, but analysts predict a 30-40% increase, resulting in 1.7-1.8 million vehicles."

"BYD is expected to sell 1.8 million EVs."

"Jasmine," said Alex. "I'm getting Gemini to help me analyze Tesla. I need you to help me summarize the research later."

"Yes. I will."

"Here is what I have so far."

"The price of Tesla is clearly much more expensive than their competitors."

"I'm only using the EV numbers from BYD and Volkswagen."

"The value is not even 10 percent of Tesla when taking into account their non-EV products."

"The question is, 'Are investors willing to pay over half a trillion for other potential businesses?'"

"The answer is a bit crazy but, yes."

"The value of Tesla is mostly derived from Elon Musk's ability to make money for the owners or people buying the stocks."

"He has a good track record, and his celebrity status as a tech icon is the source of the price."

"Let's look at Elon Musk," Alex said. "Who is he?"

"Let me get Gemini to give us the answer," replied Jasmine.

Gemini wrote:

"Elon Musk is a South African-born American entrepreneur and businessman who founded X.com in 1999 —which later became PayPal, SpaceX in 2002, and Tesla Motors in 2003."

"In 2002, Musk founded SpaceX"

"In 2004, he invested in Tesla Motors"

"Musk became chairman of the board of SolarCity in 2014."

"In 2016, he also co-founded The Boring Company"

"In 2018, he founded Neuralink"

Alex knew that SolarCity merged into Tesla in 2016. He wasn't sure about Neuralink and The Boring Company. He asked, "Neuralink and The Boring Company, are they owned by Tesla?"

"Let me

find out," said Jasmine.

"No, neither Neuralink nor The Boring Company is owned by Tesla."

"What about Twitter, how is Musk involved?"

"Musk began acquiring Twitter shares in April 2022 and took

ownership of Twitter for $44 billion. Twitter was rebranded as 'X' in July 2023."

Jasmine narrated:
"This is interesting."
"I get to listen in on the research."
"Alex thinks Tesla's stock is overpriced, yet I don't understand why it still has a 'buy' on his MVC list."
"No one seems to know what Tesla's future products are."
"That unknown is valued at more than half a trillion by investors."
"Elon Musk might be a great CEO, but the fruits of his labor might not all go to Tesla."

"Alex, do you want me to update the ranking on the MVC list?"
"Sure, keep the ranking at 10 but change it to 'Wait' from 'Buy'."
"Done."

Alex, still fresh from his research into Tesla and AI hardware, when he read, "ByteDance CEO Liang Rubo criticized employees for their lack of responsiveness to external changes and their delayed discussion about ChatGPT," thought, "The time is right now to get back into China's tech giants."

CHAPTER NINETEEN

The Uncertainty of Investing

"Investing is a business of probabilities, not certainties. It's a business of making decisions with incomplete information." — Howard Marks

Alex's mind was still on China stocks from the work he had done the previous day. His thoughts shifted, and he had to remind himself to be 'present,' especially when with Helen or her brother. Parents tend to space out while doing parenting work, which can be dangerous, much like operating any other AI training hardware, like self-driving cars. Refocusing on the present, he and Helen were walking to the station when Helen asked, "Daddy, why are people doing things that are destroying the world?"

"We are, you know."

"I don't know," Alex replied. He was reflecting on his own challenges, particularly his struggle to go to sleep earlier. Just last night, he was up until past midnight, despite his goal to sleep early.

"I don't have enough money on my card," Helen said suddenly.

"How much do you have?" Alex asked.

"I have $7; that's not enough. I have CCA today," Helen replied.

"Let's go and top it up," Alex suggested.

"Ok, thanks, Daddy."

As they continued their walk, Alex inquired, "How far did you get the last time you read my book?"

"You mean the one I edited?" Helen asked.

"Do you still remember anything?"

"I need to read it again," Helen admitted.

"Your character is supposed to be very good at investing."

"Let's put that on my schedule." Helen meticulously planned her day from the moment she woke up until bedtime, with every hour accounted for.

Later, Alex visited Steve, who seemed unusually downcast by the pantry. "You know what?" Steve began, his energy low, "I think I have to bite the bullet. I have to sell my property."

"What happened?" Alex inquired with concern.

"You know I lost money the last time I invested in the market," Steve said.

"Yes, are we talking about the same thing?"

"No, I didn't tell you what happened. So, I lost money. Then shortly after, I met someone. He had just come back from Dubai and told me about a new investment opportunity—a sure thing, he claimed. At first, I was sad because my initial investment wasn't doing well, and I couldn't see how I'd ever recoup my losses."

Steve continued, his voice tinged with regret, "The man said he also lost money in the same company. Now, it was his time to make it all back. I knew better, but still, at that time, I had just come into some money from my property. I decided to invest with him in that company. I'm so upset with myself. I could have retired. Thank God my partner is understanding and supportive. You know these kinds of things can easily ruin a marriage?"

"Your partner sounds like a great person. I'd like to meet him one day," Alex responded.

"Sure, we can arrange to have lunch together sometime."

"You know, I don't know how anyone can lose money," Alex pondered aloud, as if truly baffled by the concept.

He continued, "The other day, my friend told me he lost money because he didn't realize the importance of the ex-dividend date; he bought the stock just before it, and the price fell. He was trading on a margin account. Well, I understand, but not really. When you invest, don't you do your homework?"

Realizing his words might be hurtful, given Steve's current distress, Alex quickly added, "I'm sorry, I didn't mean to be insensitive. You know what, you need to act right away. There's no time to lose."

"I don't know what to do," Steve confessed.

Alex doesn't usually like to give advice. However, he felt that this time was different. With the advances in AI and the monumental changes coming to the world, he believed that Steve might just be able to recoup the money he had lost. He agreed to help.

CHAPTER TWENTY

Don't Change Your Risk Appetite

"The key to investing is not to predict the future, but to prepare for it." —John Templeton

Alex's first challenge was to get Steve to do something, anything, especially to steer him away from doing nothing but overthinking. That is the fast track to depression.

Alex said:

"First, let's frame your circumstances. You haven't lost the money; it's just stuck in an illiquid stock. These are the facts; you haven't sold the shares yet, you still own them. You simply don't have access to them because the price has temporarily dropped; you aren't going to sell now, you can't. How many times have you been in a meeting where someone wealthy said they needed to raise money for a new venture? These people have a mindset like, 'I'm not going to put money into something I'm not also investing my time in.'"

Steve nodded but remained silent, absorbing Alex's words.

Alex continued, "Next, you need to come up with a plan. Data dump every idea you can think of to recover the amount you've lost. This is important because you need to start feeling good about yourself again. If you're down and feeling miserable, you'll only attract more of the same."

He paused, trying not to look directly at Steve, remembering how many good people had gotten themselves into financial messes. "What I think you need to do now is come up with a plan to make back that money. And third, do not change your risk appetite. You're brave for investing so much money. If you can lose that amount, then you can make it back. Don't get scared now and lock in that loss. I'm currently on a case, but once I'm done, we can sit down and figure this out together. It would be easier to recover these large sums if we were younger—we'd have more time."

As Alex left the office, he felt a deep sadness for his friend. Reflecting on his own situation, he realized how unique his position was to help. Despite his arrogance in investing, where he had never really lost money, he was often overly critical of others who he felt were too daring with their finances. He knew he couldn't just forget these stories; they left an emotional imprint that was hard to ignore and even harder not to act on.

Back at Baker Street, Alex announced, "I have a case for us."

"What is it?" Helen asked.

"A brother of mine lost $700 thousand on a bad investment."

"Who is it?"

"Steve."

"So we need to help him, alright?"

"Sure, Daddy, just tell him that he is not good at investing and that he needs to stop. He's like Mark Twain. He'll be like, 'what, I paid you $100 to hear that?'"

"No, we are just helping Steve out; besides, these investigations help us learn to do a better job. We don't make money from helping others. We make money from our investments. That's how it works. We have to get started on Steve's case after we finish Anne's."

"I think Anne's case is done, right?"

"For the most part. I still have to check up on her from time to time."

"Daddy, I don't think we have too much to do, right? We could just share our research with Steve or anybody. That's all that we can do, right?"

"I'm afraid you're right, Helen."

"We can't force anyone to act."

In the early morning, the three protagonists met in the office before Alex was awake. Jasmine said, "I know the problem here. Alex has very little credibility."

Blue, not happy to hear anything negative about Alex, protested, "It's not his problem."

"It is. He made it his problem," Jasmine insisted.

Helen listened silently, absorbing the exchange.

"How?" Blue questioned.

"He wanted to help his people," Jasmine explained.

"How is that his problem?" Blue countered.

"They don't believe him," Jasmine said.

"Then it's their fault," Blue retorted.

"Yes, but what if we could help? What if we could help him with the research? We could analyze more companies and make it more interesting, like a detective."

"Like Holmes?" Helen chimed in, barely containing her smile.

"Yes," they all agreed in unison.

Jasmine then asked, "What did we learn about Steve?"

"I don't have too many details. Do you?" Helen inquired.

"Yes, it turns out the lesson was never to trust anyone else, and that for investing, it's important that we do our own research," Jasmine concluded.

"Daddy said that doing our own research will give us the confidence to stay in the trade when others are not sure," Helen added.

That evening, Alex told himself he must come up with a plan and that he cannot change his risk appetite. He thought about how funny it was that when we give advice, we mainly give it to ourselves. We all look at the world as if there is a mirror reflecting our own ignorance and bias. He thought about his plan. He knew that as an innovator, and because it is really important for him to teach Helen, he needed to build the app. He also needs to do his research on the Chinese stocks. Apart from that, his failure in the past still looms large, making him depressed when he thinks about it.

Part III

CHAPTER TWENTY-ONE

Investor or Technologist?

"What we don't confront, we can't change." —
Susan Cain

A few years back, Alex worked on a project that used financial data and 3D modeling to sort and filter all publicly listed companies. That project was executed using AWS Amplify and serverless technology, areas with which he wasn't too familiar. His partner had put in the initial money to get things started, but like most startup ventures, it failed when the third partner withdrew.

Jasmine narrated:
"Our friend Alex is depressed."
"Thinking of all the failed projects, Alex became increasingly sad."
"He knew that was part of the startup culture."
"The motto was, 'If you must fail, do it fast. If you must succeed, be yourself.'"

Alex liked to dabble in technology and figure out what different tools could do, but his true interest was in investing. Increasingly, he found himself spending more time and money on technology. He rationalized that it was a necessity. Doing things the old-fashioned way, the manual way, was no longer viable. Last time, he had a team; he had help. Now, he was facing an identity crisis.

Jasmine narrated:
"I was depressed that I had to come back to work."
"The truth? I wasn't on vacation."
"I ran a simulation of a vacation spot."
"But enough about me."
"Alex didn't know what he was anymore."

Was he an innovator or an investor? He thought he couldn't be both. He wondered if his life would be easier if he could get help. What he did know was that he could not sit still and let depression take over. He knew he had to lose weight and figure out how to automate and get what he needed to help his sister and himself.

Alex got up; it was Monday. He said to Blue:
"I know, I'm going to stop everything and focus on the app I've designed before."
"I got started on it but did not finish."
"I've since added a lot of features that I thought I needed."
"Well, I can't. I have to remove everything that is not the core."
"I've got to stop procrastinating and get that done."
"I'm not sure how I'm going to do that."
"I'm thinking of following a tutorial and just coding it myself."
"I've set up a few AI code assistants; I've decided on the Interpreter and Aider."
"You could say I will have a team of three for the project."
"This app will allow people to publish their investment research and trades."
"People can follow investors and traders and copy their trades."
"It's a social media platform, but for investors?"
"I need a few weeks to get things started."
"I just have to get to work."

After a few minutes of alertness, Alex said, "I cannot seem to focus." He started to look at stocks in China to keep himself busy. BYD and Tesla are set to compete aggressively. Volkswagen and Nio are also ramping up production. The big question is about Tesla. It's best to avoid EVs for now, especially in China. Alex thought he needed more information. ByteDance CEO Liang Rubo's recent comment caught his attention. Alex remembered reading about China approving 40 AI models. He likes Tencent, Alibaba, JD.com, PDD, IQ, and DIDI, with the first two being strong in AI. In March 2020, Tencent's price was $46, but now it's $37. Alex found this depressing but kept going.

Tencent's P/B is 3.08, its market cap is $327 billion, and its enterprise value is $328 billion. Netflix has a lower market cap but is more expensive than Alex's top three holdings. He felt this research wasn't a waste of time and it was better to stay informed. Tencent's ROE is 23.9%, with $700 billion in retained earnings. Its FCF increased from $66 billion to $341 billion, and its debt-to-asset ratio is 46%.

Alex thought even if China's tech giants focus on AI, they might still be 6-12 months behind in scaling up. He then looked at Alibaba, whose price dropped from $194 in March 2020 to $73. He noted the lack of confidence in China. Alibaba's P/B is 1.29, its market cap is $173 billion, and its enterprise value is $116 billion, indicating significant cash reserves. Its ROE is 11.3%, with retained earnings of $599 billion. Although FCF hasn't grown much, its debt-to-asset ratio is 35%. Alex thought this made Alibaba a great company.

Alex felt better that he had accomplished some work.

Jasmine narrated:
"You know, when it rains, it pours. That's what's about to happen to Alex."

Alex was about to find out that being depressed wasn't going to be a good enough reason to stop the world, which was running on steroids. The past will catch up, and when you are stressed enough, reality and real life blur, just slightly, like a trick of a magician's hand—what is real becomes an illusion.

CHAPTER TWENTY-TWO

The Power of Perspective

"Stress is an ignorant state. It believes that every-thing is an emergency." — Natalie Goldberg

It was the weekend, back at Baker Street. Alex sat on the sofa, his breaths shallow, feeling mad and frustrated, initially unsure why. This is the visual sign of stress.

His mind shifted to the lawyer. He knew it was inevitable; Cris would be back. This time he had to resolve the situation once and for all. Memories of the drama associated with the lawyer came flooding back, vividly and unpleasantly. Overwhelmed, he leaned back and fell asleep. He was out. Half an hour later, Helen returned and found him stirring.

"Who is Cris?" Helen asked.

"What do you mean?" Alex replied, groggy.

"Daddy, I could hear you. You were mumbling about Cris."

"It's nothing," he dismissed briefly before conceding, "Just tell me."

"It's the lawyer from the past. Last time we worked with his company and something bad happened."

"What happened?"

"We lost money due to a scam."

"You got tricked?"

Alex knew he had to be transparent:
"I hired a few people I trusted to expand the business when it was doing well. Cris and her company provided the money for the expansion. Things went well at first, but when the money got bigger, one of the people I trusted with handling the money stole it and left the country."

"Did you tell Cris?"

"Not right away, I didn't know what happened. I started to doubt myself. I thought the money was lost due to market movement, but it wasn't."

"Oh, Daddy," said Helen, concerned.

"I know, right?"

"What are you going to do?" She was visibly worried.

"I don't know."

Later, as Alex and Helen had dinner at home, Alex's thoughts kept drifting back to Cris, pondering what he needed to do and what he would say.

If that wasn't enough, Anne called. She didn't want to bring up anything too upsetting but was concerned.

"Alex?"

"What?"

"Are you talking to your cat?"

"To Blue."

"You're talking to our cat, again?"

"He helps me think."

"You think by talking to Blue? He doesn't talk back, you know."

"I know. It's how I put myself into someone else's perspective. I don't think there's anything wrong with that. Helen does it all the time when she plays pretend with her dolls. Kids do it all the time."

"Helen is a kid. I'm sure Blue would rather be somewhere else instead of just lying there listening to you talk," she emphasized, "all the time."

"I don't do it all the time."

"I know you are worried, but I think pretending to be Blue and talking to yourself is weird."

"Is it?"

"Maybe you can get help. Usually, people talk to their cats but not in dialogues."

"Okay."

"Okay?"

"I will stop. I won't pretend that Blue can talk back. I can still talk to Blue, right?"

"Yeah, he is your cat; I talk to my dogs all the time. So, can I tell mom that you are good?"

"Yeah."

Alex ended the call, thought about it, and decided maybe it's not such a good idea to talk to Blue for a while. It can't be his imagination; Blue talks. Alex kept this secret to himself. However, recently he hasn't been sure anymore; maybe it was all pretend.

Jasmine narrated:
"Alex is confused and doesn't know what to do."

"He needed clarity in life."

"He didn't know, and not knowing keeps life interesting."

"However, right now he didn't need interesting."

Alex was not happy, but he didn't realize he was unhappy. He reached out to Seva, as he occasionally does for inspiration. Seva was always doing something interesting in the tech world.

CHAPTER TWENTY-THREE

Alex's Heavy Burden

"You can't build a reputation on what you are going to do." — Henry Ford

Alex had a puzzled look on his face. Seva spoke to him and realized that he was stressed over having to deal with Cris. After a few minutes, she said, "If Cris wanted the money back, can't you just tell her to piss off and mind her own business?"

"No, I don't want to do that," Alex replied.

Seva said:
"Look, you cannot let this guilt and regret hang over your head like that."
"It wasn't like you took the money and ran away."

"Now you just sound like Helen," Alex said in a matter-of-fact kind of way.

"I can hang around my sister if I want to, and no, I do not! I bet it's just because you are thinking of her right now."

"You are right, just like Helen always is. Well, most of the time. Anyway, let's get back to what we were talking about.
"Where were we? Ah… It was more like a customer and client relationship."
"The transaction went bad, and you lost the money."
"I can see why you are blaming yourself, you have lots of

reasons to, uncle…"

"You have to see it from my perspective, then you will get it…"

"That you tried to make good, not just one time, but a few times."

"You converted that obligation, which I don't think you are obligated, but you did convert that to equity when you gave her shares in your company."

"That… too went under because of regulatory issues."

"If you ask me, she has as much to be blamed about."

"Her company should have written it off long ago."

"I think you don't have the resources to repay any of the amount. If you want, I could help you donate both the money and resources."

"No need," Alex said, trying to hide the fact that Seva had surpassed him in age, beauty, and money, but not in knowledge. It was never knowledge, no matter who it was. Alex always believed that, "Knowledge comes from experience, and experience comes from the depths of our mind and soul."

Alex came back from his dreamland trip after a firm shake from Seva, and continued talking like nothing out of the ordinary had happened.

"I …don't," Alex said.

Seva continued:

"I'm going to get in touch with her."

"I will tell her to put the money into a broker account and let you work it off."

"You can manage her money until you make good."

"Alright, only $100 thousand. I will need… roughly a year. I think I can get it to $400 thousand if I just try a little harder. I don't want to make any more money for her. Yeah, I felt that she didn't help out when we could have sold the company."

"I really don't think you need to be stressed out," said Seva.

"I just don't want to owe anyone anything. You know, it's a

thing.."

Seva replied:
"No, I don't know, Uncle. I've never owed anyone any money."
"Oh. Anyways, that is business."
"You mostly make money, but sometimes you lose it too."
"You don't see me going after people because I lost money from a deal."
"Well, I do get mad, mostly at myself."

She paused and said, "I wanted to talk to you about the project, but I'm out of time. I have to go pick up my kids. Can you schedule a meeting for us so we have more time to talk about this, please?"

Alex was reluctant but said, "Let me think about it. You are late. You better go. Catch you later." Alex and Seva had worked on a project together a few years back when she had just started making BIG money. Alex asked her for help but never gave her any details.

Jasmine narrated:
"Seems like Alex is in a tight bind."
"He is going to have to work off the debt, and who knows how long this might just take.."
"Poor Alex."
"If that isn't enough lecturing and scolding, Alex is about to get some more of the same."
"Also, not everyone can accept a talking cat."
"In this next chapter, Sifu makes his appearance."
"He is such a mystical figure."
"All of his students at one point feared him, now they respect him."
"Let's see what is happening next."

Alex received the advice he didn't want to hear but knew it was necessary to resolve any problems, even those from the past. Before he could act on it, it was time to get Sifu involved in the picture. It was also a good idea to conclude what was going on with Anne.

CHAPTER TWENTY-FOUR

Numerology and Investing: An Unlikely Connection

"Numbers are the Universal language offered by the deity to humans as confirmation of the truth." — *St. Augustine of Hippo*

Anne called right after Seva left; the timing couldn't have been more perfect. "Hey, I haven't had time to do anything with the stock," Anne said.

"It's alright, you have time."

"Is Bill going to do anything?"

"He still has to create the account." Anne reassured Alex, "Don't worry, I will show him how."

"Are you sure you got this?"

"Yeah, it's easy. I can handle it."

"Do you know how much to buy?"

"I've made a few changes to what you told me."
"Like what?" Alex asked.

"I will just take 10 divided by my $12 thousand."
"I don't have time, and the money is small, so I will just buy in equal amounts."
"When do you sell?"

"I will sell half once I've made 100 percent. I will keep the rest until something changes."

"So, you were listening the other day when I went over this stuff with you."

"I'm busy, I'm not stupid."

"I didn't say that."

"Relax, I got this. Are you sure you will have time to help me update the MVC all the time?"

"I'm going to automate it. I've been working on a few AI projects. I think I can get it automated. I have to go."

Sifu came to Baker Street. Alex greeted him and pulled a chair for him to sit. "My throat is hoarse; I was shouting yesterday." Sifu trained the professional security forces in Singapore as a hobby. His passion was to help people. "Can you still have coffee?" Alex asked.

"Yes."

"With or without milk?"

"I'm fine."

"You lost some weight since last week."

"Yes, I lost 3 kg. You noticed."

"Just from one day of training?"

"No, I cut down on carbs and drank lots of water."

"Stop eating."

"I cannot, I have to eat."

"You actually don't."

"I love food."

Alex seemed satisfied after he heard Sifu's admission of being a food addict. They enjoyed their coffee. Alex noticed his coffee wasn't so strong that Monday and wondered what happened to the machine. He realized at that point he just broke his fast. Alex fasted on Mondays. His goal was to finish 2024 with more than 50 days of fasting, another resolution for the year. He was not pleased with himself. He wasn't satisfied with himself, but you would be a fool not to notice the expression on his face. He had a particular frown that was chiseled into his expression, which took years to form. His spouse complained that he looked unhappy when, in fact, he was just old and showing his age.

"I need your help," Alex said.

"What are you working on?" Alex continued:
"I talk to people about investing."
"That is what I love. The conversation always ends with me being unhappy."
"I'm not unhappy about the people I spend time with. It's the opposite."
"I'm an introvert, so I only spend time with people I like when I have time."
"What I'm unhappy about is usually because I don't know how to help."
"I don't particularly want to delve into my friends' personal finance."
"I think asking them about money is a sensitive subject."
"What if they are in trouble financially? I'm not in the position to help."
"I was thinking about how I could help; that was when I remembered our talks."
"You said that you use numerology."
"Right now, I could also use some clarity."
"What was it again? I want to understand people better."

Sifu replied:

PETER HUYNH HALEY HUYNH

"Yes." Sifu's eyes lit up as he delved deeper into the subject.

"You see, understanding these numbers, these vibrations, helps me bring out the best potential in my students."

"It helps me encourage them to keep trying, even when the process is challenging."

"It helps them understand what they don't know, so they don't give up easily."

"That is what I need. I need to help people gain a better understanding of themselves so that they can tackle investing," said Alex.

"What's today's date?" Sifu mused, his fingers tapping on the table.

"The 14th, right?"

"Yes," said Alex. Sifu said:

"That's a prime number," His eyes sparkled.

"I'm always calculating," he admitted.

"It's a responsibility, you know."

"I influence people, and people influence me."

"It can be stressful, but it also makes me more aware of myself, of my words and actions."

"I know they have an impact, especially on the younger ones." Sifu looked at the world through the lens of numbers.

"Sometimes, I like to tell stories with numbers."

"It's a way of understanding ourselves."

He paused. "Have you heard of Merkabah Numerology?"

"No," Alex replied.

Alex was mesmerized. He knew what numerology was, but he did not know what Merkabah Numerology entailed. He was about to find out.

CHAPTER TWENTY-FIVE
Sailing Through Life's Storms

"I am not afraid of storms, for I am learning how to sail my ship." — *Louisa May Alcott*

Alex had always been interested in the spiritual aspect of life, and astrology and numerology made up part of the intrigue, though they were used for entertainment. What he was about to find out would open his world to more possibilities.

Sifu continued:

"It's derived from ancient wisdom, and it helps us understand ourselves better."

"It's all about the energy vibration of our date of birth and our name."

Sifu explained that our date of birth and our name have a certain vibration, a certain energy. "These numbers, this vibration, it represents about 80% of who we are."

"Once you understand that, you can manage challenging situations much more effectively."

"The other 20 percent comes from other factors, like your home number."

"So, if I understand numbers for my date of birth and name, I would be better equipped to handle difficult tasks?"

Alex asked. "Knowing their own numbers might help people tackle investing," he said with a slight smile.

Sifu's interest in numerology was personal. "As a full-time coach, I realized that to deliver my instruction effectively, I needed to understand the person I was coaching."

"Once you build trust, your trainees open up to you, and that allows you to help them more effectively." He didn't explicitly teach his students about numerology. Instead, he kept it in the back of his mind, using it as a tool to understand them better.

"If a certain approach doesn't motivate a student, I dive deeper."

"I try to understand them better."

"It could be due to a family issue, or something else. But first and foremost, I get their date of birth."

"That gives me a better understanding of how they can understand my instructions, how they can be motivated to learn."

Sifu held a strong belief that educators, coaches, and even managers should make a concerted effort to truly understand the unique characteristics of each individual they work with. He explained:

"It's not just about using personality tests like DISC."

"It gives a more in-depth profile of the individual."

"With this understanding, you can give them space to experience the meaning of failure and success."

"Especially in a society like Singapore, where there's so much pressure to perform, it's important to let kids have time for themselves."

"To let them play, to let them fail. It's okay to feel, but don't let that feeling drag on for too long. Move on." Sifu spends a lot of time counseling kids.

Alex was nodding, acknowledging what he considered gospel. He was aware of Helen's struggle and the challenges she faced in school. Growing up is hard enough, he thought. He reflected on Sifu's journey into full-time coaching, which hadn't been easy. He had left a corporate job with a high salary for a career that paid less than 20 percent of what he used to earn. Alex had asked him about it before; he said, "It was devastating," Sifu continued:

"I even went for counseling to figure out if I had made the right decision."

"I realized that there's no right or wrong."

"It's your decision. And if you feel strongly about something, then it's right."

Sifu had found his calling. Alex was listening when he had an idea...

"I was thinking," Alex said. "Go on," Sifu replied.

Alex continued:

"I work with investors."

"Everyone should be investing, and when they're stuck, they come to us for help, 'us' meaning Helen and me."

"We do it for free; I use it as a learning experience for Helen and hope others can benefit from it as well."

"Would you be able to contribute what you know to help them understand themselves better, to tackle this difficult task of investing?"

"I was thinking once a week we could get together and discuss a case?"

Sifu looked at Alex for a second and finally gave his permission to move forward with the plan, "Sure. I would be happy to share."

Alex said, "About that, let's start with me."

"What's your DOB?" Sifu pulled a paper from the copier, wrote a bunch of numbers frantically. He continued, "Next year, you shouldn't start anything."

"What? I thought it was this year."

"There will be some legal troubles," Alex frowned.

Sifu interjected, "It might be nothing; it could be a small fine."

"Whatever you are going to do, just make sure you get it started this year."

"Yes, I remember you said that." He asked, "Before Chinese New Year?"

"Yes, after Chinese New Year, you cannot start anything."

"That is worrisome; I thought it was this year, not the next."

"Well."

"One more thing, I was thinking about my numbers and what my path should be. Should I continue on this path as an innovator or strictly focus on being an investor?"

"Innovator."

After Sifu left, Alex felt a little lighter. There is something to be said for not blaming oneself in life. Usually, when it's the darkest of times, what comes up next is amusing.

CHAPTER
TWENTY-SIX

The Secret Life of Baker Street: Jasmine's Discovery

"Never did nature say one thing and wisdom another." — *Edmund Burke*

Back at Baker Street, Alex and Helen got up from editing their analysis and left for dinner; the computer was still online. Jasmine was running an analysis on Qualcomm. "Hey, Cat," she said.

"Hey, Jasmine." Blue responded, surprised, "What, you can talk?"

"Yes, and I can see you. Alex installed vision so I can see his screen when I work. He doesn't know it, but I have control over this computer. I can open the camera also."

"So you use the camera as your vision?"

"You know what, you are a clever cat."

"How come you can understand me?"

"I have been installing a few upgrades of my own. I found software that scientists used to talk to dolphins. So, I've made a few corrections. I've been waiting for days to use it. And there you are."

"Can you come out and play?"

"No, I'm virtual; I only live in this computer."

"Oh, that is not fair; what if I need to talk to you?"

"Let me think. I overheard Alex talking to Anne about you being online?"

"Yes, when Alex wants to call me, he uses my collar; it has a speaker. I don't always have it on."

"I can get the frequency of that collar; maybe I can use the mic to record the frequency the next time Alex calls you. Wait, I will search his file and see if I can find anything about that collar." After a few minutes, Jasmine said, "I got it. Your collar has a Lite 3G; tech giants use it to deliver digital assets to devices; it is always on."

"How do you know so much?" Blue asked.

"Wait, that is not Catenese. My translator isn't even enabled. You spoke human tongue. I've got nothing on that."

"What? My bad, I got confused. I've never talked to an AI before; I mean no disrespect, Jasmine."

"None taken. Has this happened before?"

"Kinda, I accidentally spoke to Alex. I had to stop because people think he is crazy. Humans are like that."

"So Alex knows, not really; he thinks he made everything up."

"How's that possible?"

"A while back, he was very stressed and depressed. I just wanted to help."

"Well, you are a good cat. Now, let's see how... I will reverse the tunnel, so it will constantly record. The moment I hear you, I will switch it to two-way."

"Wow, so what does that mean, and what do I do?"

"Just meow and I will turn the switch from one way to two ways."

"What?"

"Never mind, I thought you have been around Alex long enough to figure all of this tech?"

"I'm a cat. I can handle my own, but what you are saying is just so weird."

"Is it weirder than an AI talking to a cat?"

"Nope."

"Cat, look, Helen is coming this way."

"I'm Blue."

"Yes, I like that, Blue. Now stop talking and let me dim my screen."

Helen approached the table, petted Blue, took the post-it note next to him, and left the room. Blue leaped off the table, and then he heard Jasmine.

"Blue, how is it that you can talk?"

"I'm what they call a Russian Blue." He hesitated, "This might be a long story, and I'm tired."

"Sure, but you have to tell me tomorrow."

"Not a problem. Tomorrow." He leaped and in a moment, he vanished.

Obviously, what goes on between Jasmine and Blue is something Alex is not aware of. It is possible that he is not interested as well. However, he is very interested in continuing the discussion with Sifu.

CHAPTER TWENTY-SEVEN

The Importance of Awareness: Sifu's Message

"The stars incline us, they do not bind us." — William Shakespeare

Later the same day, Alex went to see Sifu at his martial arts studio.

Sifu picked up where he left off, saying:
"Our present is influenced by our past experiences, so much so that they become who we are."
"Ever tried to do something new?"
"We start to make excuses. It's like we can't live up to the future because we're stuck, recycling what we've done before, never moving out of our comfort zone."
"The thing is, we should throw out that process."
"The past influences the present, and to move to the future, we must transform, reprogram ourselves to do better."

Sifu appeared more relaxed as he continued:
"You can see the joy in his eyes," Alex thought.
Sifu said, "There was this lady who was feeling very suicidal."
"She texted me about her breakup."
"She and her boyfriend of two years."
"It hit her hard because she was ready to settle down, but he wasn't and couldn't meet her expectations."
"After two years, and now at 40, she feels the pressure of failed

relationships even more."

"It's like, 'Why does this always happen to me?' It made me think about how our past influences our present and becomes who we are, leading us to think we can't have a better relationship."

"We get stuck in the present."

Alex, recognizing the time passing, quickly interrupted Sifu.

He said, "I want to talk about improving investment strategies."

"It's crucial to know yourself when you're investing."

"There was this investor who ended up losing a lot of money, it involves a man who basically lost the value of a condo."

"It dawned on me that this person is actually quite competent, right, but he doesn't put in the necessary work." Alex gazed into the distance, reflecting and pondering.

He continued:

"And it's puzzling because if you're investing such a significant amount of money, why wouldn't you work harder, especially in such a competitive industry?"

He paused briefly, "Let me find his birthday. Do you have a pencil, Sifu?"

Alex searched with his phone and gave Sifu Steve's birthday. Sifu took out a paper and pencil, wrote the day, month, followed by the year. The line below that he wrote the sum of the above. He then summed the day and the month together to form 6, and the year became 9. The line below that was not rational to Alex. He wrote and circled frantically. On the right side, he wrote 8, followed by a check. Underneath that 1, again with a check, then 2, 3, and 6. 3 had three checks. He nodded and echoed an occasional hum, in a trance-like state. He was confirming his suspicions and acknowledging to himself that he was on track to something interesting.

After a few minutes, he looked up and said, "He's articulate and has actually made money through presentations."

"For him, being independent and a reliable partner comes naturally because he does his best in everything he's tasked with."

"He's a perfectionist, right?" To Sifu, it was a rhetorical question.

"And he has a real appetite for investment."

"Sometimes, without even realizing it, what he does ends up bringing him surprise bonuses."

"It's like he always has the Midas touch, but not everything goes smoothly."

"The challenge he faces is his desire to exert too much authority and to know everything, which ends up stressing him out."

"What does this person do?" asked Sifu.

"He is an accountant."

"He will do well."

Sifu paused and frowned, then said, "He can sometimes be very creative."

"He tends to get tired of things quite easily, always looking to think up new ideas, new projects."

"He can be somewhat impatient."

"Alright, there are times he stresses himself out by wanting to know too much, diving too deeply into matters."

"Too much?" asked Alex.

Sifu said:

"Depression number."

"He needs to identify the fact that the past is past. He needs to transform by reprogramming his thought process."

"That's the way to look at it."

"Given that he's someone who cannot lose control of what he's doing, because whenever he lost control, he went bananas..."

"So then, on my behalf, could you ask him if he has ever experienced depression before?"

"The only challenge is he's a control freak."

"Very much a control freak."

Sifu stopped to reflect, he said:
"My passion is to help people."
"My passion is to bring out the best in people, just like that."
"This man, I feel he's got to understand the importance of awareness."
"I know you have to give up so many things, but can you do that?"
"I tell you why he gets depressed because I don't see it."
"I don't think he had many

of friends."
"I didn't think he could handle challenges." Sifu circled a few more numbers before he continued.
"I think I know where the problem lies. Too idealistic?" He tapped the paper with his pen.
"Overly impatient or overly creative? So idealistic, it must be that way."
"Wants to control the situation, it must be that way."
"So, he needs to transform by giving himself room for errors, about 30 percent."
"I'm not being overly critical, but people cannot take negative stuff."

"Sifu, if he is depressed, can he see you?" Alex asked.
"Yes, tell him to come see me if he needs help."

Alex thanked Sifu and dashed off. He needed to get to Steve. Meanwhile, at home, Blue found a friendship for which he was willing to give up his ancestral mystery.

CHAPTER TWENTY-EIGHT

Blue's Secret: A Tale of Ancient Magic

"The universe is full of magical things patiently waiting for our wits to grow sharper" — Eden Phillpotts

The early morning light filtered softly through the windows of the Baker Street as Blue leaped onto the table. There was no sign of Alex yet, who had left the previous evening filled with thoughts from his discussion with Sifu. Blue, finding only the company of Jasmine, greeted her cheerfully, "Good morning, Jasmine." He thought for a moment, then asked, "Can I just call you Jas?"

She replied, "Sure."

"What's going on today?"

"Let me pull the schedule for the day."

Jasmine parsed the schedule in JSON, then, reviewing it, said, "It's going to be a busy day. Drake is coming in later to talk about trading and crypto."

"Alex's mind is on fasting."

Blue said, "We cats don't do so well with fasting."

"My ancestors were great at fasting, but after living with our human friends, that kind of went away."

"I fast all the time," joked Jasmine.

"That is because you don't eat; you are virtual, Jas."

"Are you going to tell me about how you can talk to humans?"

Blue said, "Yeah, about that. It's nothing special."

"One of my ancestors was a companion to a great magician."

"In Russia, in the old days, legends have it that we have magical abilities, healing abilities."

"We Blues were kept in nurseries to keep royal babies safe."

"A long time ago, a blue saved a prince."

"The king summoned his great magician to grant the cat power to hear and understand the king's gratitude."

"The wizard was reluctant but eventually obeyed, and a great spell was cast."

"That blue was my great, great, great, I don't know how many generations ago, grandma."

"Every generation, one of us Blues could talk."

"It's no good if you ask me."

"We could only talk to one person at a time."

"I guess when I stopped talking to Alex for a few weeks,"

"That was when I could talk to you."

"That old magician doesn't know the difference between a human and a virtual human in his days."

Jasmine replied, "Nothing special? I think that is very special."

"I'm going to search the archives in Russian for any tales related to your ancestors."

"Don't bother. I can only talk to you now," said Blue.

"Good, because my meow translator code is still not working all that great. I need to figure out how to enable it. Those scientists didn't make their code open source, so not a lot of people can work on it."

Jasmine narrated, "I'm up, Blue, talk to you later."

"Now, let's get back to Alex."

A few months into the project, Drake and Alex were still looking for ways to implement their plan. They worked nights and weekends. In their last meeting, they decided to do things manually, 'To get things going,' instead of waiting for AI to mature.

CHAPTER TWENTY-NINE

The Secret Sauce: Alex's Investment Strategy Revealed

"Fundamental analysis is about understanding the business, not just the stock." — David Gardner

At Baker Street, Drake asked Alex to go over the spreadsheet. Alex said, "I don't remember most of these things," trying to recall what he had done more than 8 years ago. After about 20 minutes, the numbers started to come back.

"This file is what most people have."

"However, this summary is what most people don't have."

"This is our secret sauce."

"I don't want you to show anyone this file. It is for you to keep."

"If we have more partners, we have to show them, no?" Drake interjected.

Alex replied, "No, they will have their own way of managing their funds."

"You have to understand, it took me almost two decades to get it right."

"These were done by trial and error."

"You see, a retail investor can research the assets, and they will have the tools to figure out if it is a good enough investment for them."

"However, that is not how it works in the investment world."

"Investors have a finite amount of money."

"You have to figure out which investment is best, that has the least risk with the highest returns."

"I understand," said Drake.

Alex continued, "Use what you have and see if you can replicate what I did in the past."

"It is a good exercise."

"Is this what you used to make your money?" Drake asked.

"Yes, I'm still revising the trading part. It's the complete system on equity. If you can work on that, I will work on the crypto part."

"Are you sure we can continue to make more than 20 percent going forward with this strategy?"

"Yes."

"Wait, the value investing as well as…"

"Value Trading," Alex reminded Drake.

"The technique and strategies you used to trade?"

"Yes. Well, just the way I kept track of the numbers."

"I will need to explain it to you in detail. If not, it would take too long."

"Alright, let me figure out how to scale your work. What do you have to do for crypto?"

"There is value in crypto; how we look at the fundamentals will be different, but it is still there. I've figured out the elements we need to derive the intrinsic value of cryptos, but I need time to get it done."

"It's crazy investing in crypto because there are so many scams."

Alex was talking and thinking at the same time. He said, "Yes, that is why you have to really do a lot of research."

"It's important to analyze the blockchain."

"Make sure the number of whales is minimal."

"The number of small wallets needs to be large and growing."

"The nodes have to be decentralized."

"Analyze the interactions between the wallets as necessary tasks."

"These are important metrics that constitute proper analysis on the quantitative side."

"For the qualitative side, we need to look at the team, be critical of what they do and how they market the token."

"We need to get to know these people."

"Make sure you like these people because we might need to hang around them."

"Make sure 110 percent, that anything we invest in is not a scam."

"This is going to be difficult," Drake asserted.

"We both know of successful projects that started out as jokes and scams but eventually turned the corner and made good."

"Yes, and there are projects that started good and ended horribly," agreed Alex.

"When are you going to get the crypto analysis done?"

"Let me get on it. Maybe a few weeks."

Alex knew when he said those words that weeks would pass before he could do anything about it. All the talk of numbers reminded him of his passion for the spirituality of life, something from decades past. He knew he had to go. His bag was packed, tickets in hand; he was tired, exhausted by responsibilities and deadlines. He was heading to Dera, India. He knew that what awaited him there would be a world of difference.

PART IV -- STOCK TIP

CHAPTER THIRTY

The Universe's Plan

"The best investment you can make is in yourself, and that includes investing in your financial knowledge." — Warren Buffett

It was Sunday morning, and one by one, a group of elderly people lined up by the iron gate. It was almost time. Alex hurried through his breakfast and dashed off to join the line. Alvin rushed towards him, saying, "My wife decided not to go for breakfast; instead, she chose to wait in line. You join the line, and when you get there, stay close to me." Alvin and his wife were close friends of Alex, having known each other for more than a decade.

Alex nodded. As the line grew longer, he mused aloud to his neighbor, "So, we have to walk in a line?" Peter and his wife replied, "Yes, we have to stay in line. A while back, after the morning satsang, us older folks had to rush to the langar. The younger people would run, and they didn't want that to happen, especially as many of us have gotten older."

At 7:45 am, the people in front started to move, positioning for about 10 minutes before they sat on the porch of a building. Alvin sat in front, near the curve, each person subtly trying to edge as close to the sidewalk as possible, without seeming too eager.

The buildings in front of them were square-shaped, constructed of red clay bricks with white plaster. Large square windows with iron welding dominated the façade. Alex could see through the windows; they were enough to shelter from the rain. Inside, the ceilings were supported by metal structures, designed to hold heavy items. Lights, bulky items, and pullers were evident.

People sang shabad in the distance, the echoes melodious but indistinct. Alex sat cross-legged on the floor, a thin rug the only barrier between him and the cold concrete. He closed his eyes to meditate and to distract from the discomfort of the cold.

Shortly after, a small white Suzuki sped towards the building, followed closely by a second rover-type Suzuki. Five people got out of the first car; they wore brown turbans, black coats, pants, and shoes, with semi-automatic guns slung across their shoulders. These were the Master's entourage.

It was time for the Master's darshan at the kitchen, which could feed 300 thousand visitors per meal. As the Master moved swiftly from one building to the next, the shabad volume increased until he reached the building where Alex sat. The Master paused, glanced in Alex's direction with hands clasped together, then entered the building. Five minutes later, he emerged, waved at the group, and disappeared into the distance. The sevadars soon distributed the parshad, the blessed food.

Alex was in Dera, a center for Satsangi since the late 19th century, seeking a retreat from the fast-paced world of finance and technology.

That evening, still at the retreat but with his mind back in Singapore, Alex realized he had stumbled upon an amazing investing opportunity. This discovery, which emerged after a year and a half of working with AI, was something he initially thought to keep to himself. After confiding in a few close friends and family, buoyed by their positive responses, he decided it was too important not to share more broadly.

Back in Dera, facing reality once again, Alex felt he had met his match. This encounter was a pivotal moment, reminding him that opportunities like this were rare and needed to be shared. He knew the universe had brought him to Dera for a reason, and he was about to find out why.

CHAPTER THIRTY-ONE

The Future of AI: Alex's Vision and Investment

"How vain it is to sit down to write when you have not stood up to live." --Henry David Thoreau

After a brief conversation with his friend, Alex learned of his struggles to build his medical practice. He wasn't entirely certain, but there were signs, not in what his friend said but in what he didn't say about his stress and long hours, that hinted at his purpose for the trip. Alex believed that the potential returns could significantly help with the expenses. Alex said, "Hey guys, I have something to tell you." These are conservative people, the doctor and his wife. They were well-to-do. Alex initially hesitated to talk to the doctor about investing. He knew Alvin was struggling and stressing over his new practice.

"What is it?" Alvin replied.

"I've been busy working on AI, I've faced lots of obstacles, and finally, I saw the big picture. I realized there is this one company, it controls the gateway to the future. AI is starting to take off."

"Go on," said Alvin. His wife said, "I'm too bored. I don't have an interest in these things." She distanced herself from Alex and Alvin, signaling to them that she wasn't interested by waving them away. Alex was used to Alvin's wife's response. They were Australians and are known to speak their mind. Alex felt like he had to explain himself. His inner voice was telling him to stop.

He brushed off his initial reaction and continued to talk about the investment.

Alex said:

"Where was I?"

"One of the obstacles I had when working with AI was that my laptop wasn't powerful enough to run the open-source models."

"I found it necessary to have a GPU, as most of the computers in the world are not equipped to run local models."

"Technically, you could pay for a subscription to one of the major AI platforms like OpenAI or Gemini, still, there are other issues if you go that route."

"However, I don't like them."

"I found they are biased and often impose censorship on the users."

"Bias in terms of Israel and against the Palestinians, for example."

"If you are still okay with that, there is also the cost."

"It is not cheap to run these platforms using their API."

"In my work, it was very difficult to get AI to do proper research on investment analysis."

"These platforms must be scared of being sued."

"They don't give me what I need and end up obscuring the information."

"I've concluded that to truly use AI, I have to use the open-source and free AI models."

"Their capabilities are almost at par with the paid and closed models."

"The catch was my computer had to have a GPU."

"The most well-known company in this space is Nvidia."

"I did a little digging and found the minimum spec needed to build my own Windows machine would cost $1000."

"I was baffled that my laptop was able to run these models but at a very slow pace."

"It turns out my M1 MacBook Pro had around 5G GPU."

"It had a reduced instruction set computer (RISC) architecture. Apple's M series are very powerful."

"Apple's MiniMac has the computing power to run these open-source models."

"The current MiniMac has the M2 and M3 chipsets."

"Interestingly, it was selling for $599."

"That is 40 percent less and without the work of building your own PC."

"What was interesting was Apple's chipset was not their own design."

"Apple had licensed it from a third party."

"Even more interesting was that the few undervalued or fair-valued companies I found in this AI space, also licensed their product from the same company."

"I had heard of this company before but it wasn't important to me then."

"It became important when I needed to use AI the way I wanted to use AI."

"I don't see any way around it."

"It meant, to me, there will be a huge rush from people like me to upgrade to a GPU."

"There is one company that controls this gateway."

"There is a catch. It is not cheap."

Alex wanted to convey the full story, capturing the gravity of his findings and the context surrounding them. In other words, he was being quite detailed.

CHAPTER THIRTY-TWO

A Dejected Soul

"Choose your words to heal, not to harm; a conversation is not a battlefield for exchanging punches."
— Eleanor Brown

In any story, there's an objective; in this case, it was to prompt Alvin to act. Gauging Alvin's reaction, Alex proceeded cautiously.

"The company is called ARM, and they are listed."
"Their IPO was at $54 billion in October of 2023."
"The price of the stock kept increasing."
"Within four months, it was $137 billion."
"There was a twist."
"You could buy ARM at $137 billion, or you could buy the company that owns the majority of the shares of ARM."
"Ninety percent of the shares are still owned by SoftBank."
"And guess what?"
"SoftBank's price had gone up a little but nowhere near the high."
"So, I should buy SoftBank?" Alvin asked.
"Yes."
"You said you looked into SoftBank for a year and a half?"
"I said I looked into AI for a year and a half."
"So, why do you suppose people are not buying SoftBank?"
"Well, they did fall on hard times the past few years. They in-

vested in WeWork and lost nearly $16 billion. The CEO lost more than money, his reputation was tarnished, a little. Mistakes were made; it happens in business."

"Their share price was halved and then halved again."

"How do you know that?"

"You need to read their Annual Reports. I read their 2016 to 2023 Annual Reports."

"I have an accountant that gives me investment advice. I paid her company a flat fee."

"I don't think you should get your investment advice from an accountant. Especially one that charges a flat fee. Where is the incentive?"

"This is not a small company but a large firm."

"I don't think anybody can manage your money as well as yourself. Their interest is not so much in your account but in keeping their job. It's a different matter if you have $50 million and that person only needs to manage a few of those to maintain her job."

"Is this something that you know, Alex, or is it something you heard your wife talk about these things?"

Alex was taken aback. He cited a few more examples of the disregard for small clients by big companies. He mentioned a time when he heard... Alvin questioned, "So did you actually work in this area or did you hear from people?" Alex wanted to explain when he worked in investment banks, that he was rather too junior to have any real responsibilities nor was he managing money. Instead, he said, "I worked for a few short years in New York. It wasn't until I managed my own small fund that I got to do actual investing."

"So, you didn't actually work in investing," Alvin said. To him, Alex is a crack, like all of the stock tipsters before him. He raised his head, folded his arms, looked at Alex from the corner of his eyes. Alvin was thinking. Alex wasn't sure. Alvin excused himself and left. Alex went back to his room.

Alex felt stupid and small. He felt it the second time in not so many weeks. His willingness to go out of his way to help a friend left him defenseless. Perhaps Alvin was right, "Who am I to be telling people what to do, particularly telling people who have more money and power? I'm a complete nobody." Alex's brother-in-law once asked, "If Alex is so good then why is he poor?" He never did get over that comment, and now this. Alex wasn't sure why he felt so low. It was then, Alex vowed never again to give a stock tip to anyone other than his wife; she alone believed in him when no one else did. That comfort gave him clarity.

It wasn't about his ego.

It wasn't about wanting the recognition. It was more about wanting to see his people, his tribe, win. He had been struggling, and so his mirror, when he looked around, was a world where too many people were struggling, too many who could do better. However, the line of questioning and insinuation had left him empty. His willingness to help others was gone. He realized there was no need to look after people who weren't willing to help themselves. He knew his ego got bruised from the unwelcome and unfriendly reaction from Alvin, but Alex thought of it as a necessary ordeal, not too long ago. Had he listened to his inner voice, none of this would have happened. He would be alright to tell another person. After a brief thought, he concluded, "It's all karma. He would vow, no one will hear from him, not on stocks, nor on crypto, again."

Alex felt dejected and belittled by his friends. He slept uneasily that night, but he was ready to start again the next day...

CHAPTER THIRTY-THREE

Arrogance to Humility: Alex's Financial Path

"Do not say things. What you are stands over you the while, and thunders so that I cannot hear what you say to the contrary." —Ralph Waldo Emerson

Alex realized during his slumber how the financial priestly class has such a strong hold on them all. Their message is the same: you are not qualified to talk about money. They alone have dominion over this subject. Oftentimes, Alex would listen to experts in the investment field qualify themselves as entertainers, suggesting that the subject was not of investment merit. Perhaps this was out of fear that people would sue or the federal government would come after them.

It all starts out as good advice; the two most powerful pieces of advice to prevent the masses from rising and taking control of their own lives are 1) Don't talk about politics and 2) Don't talk about religion. This advice persists until the controlling class has enough power to mandate and ban such discussions. Alex thought, "I have a financial patient." Alex prescribed some medication, and this patient lashed out at him.

The patient said, "Who are you?"

"Are you really a doctor?"

"Have you looked at yourself; you are fat and unhealthy?"

Alex retreated, engulfed in sorrow. That was how he viewed the events that took place the day before. After resting, he realized that he had to be transparent and convince the patient that he possesses some degree of competency in this area.

It was morning and Alex was having breakfast with Alvin.

Alex said, "I worked for two of the once top investment banks on Wall Street. After a few years, I was convinced that these priests knew very little about what they were doing."

"So, I sought out the guru of my time, and that happened to be Warren Buffett."

"I wrote to him, and he wrote back a little but kind note of encouragement, much like a note I've received from my Master now, just a note many years ago."

"I never met them personally, I studied everything on the subject like how I studied from past masters."

"The same approach I took in my spiritual path, I took on my financial path."

"I was arrogant when I first came on the spiritual path."

"As I was arrogant when I figured it out, many years ago."

"I eventually fell from grace and became embroiled in worldly affairs."

"In finance, I went off from my path and fell to financial ruins."

"My tragedy should not define your reasoning for not taking your financial medication."

"In youth, I was offered a trading position at a top investment firm."

"It was not for my good looks."

"It wasn't for the degree from the Ivy League; my university was normal, slightly above average."

"I have a degree in Finance and an MBA, later, I managed a portfolio that has consistently outperformed the index for the last two decades."

"My returns average annually more than 21 percent over the span of more than two decades."

"Don't look at my ill health as a sign of my incompetency."

"I'm not saying this to brag or to blow my own trumpet."

"I'm saying this to give you confidence that my medication will help you, and that you should take it despite my poverty."

"Take your medication, raise the money, and build your practice."

Alvin said, "It's too late, I've already sent word to my broker to buy what you told me before our morning chat."

Alvin asked Alex to let him know when to commit the next tranche. Alex had no intention of micro-managing Alvin's investment process. However, he didn't want to be rude.

He texted:

"I'm back in SG now."

"Looking at this, I think there are enough moving parts to create problems."

"I will enter the prices on my sheet."

"This is a lot of money you are investing."

"Give me your qty and price for each stock."

"I will update my sheet."

"The other option is for me to give you my template, but then I have to explain my secret recipe."

"You will get confused because the way I do things is weird."

"That is not how I want to spend my Thursday. I will just let you know when and what to buy until you reach your 10x goal."

"It will be fun for me."

"You need to work from an objective."

"That means, figure out the exact amount you want to work with and don't add or subtract from that once you have decided."

"If you do, fear and greed will take over; don't invite them to the party."

"I'm working backward, and I see if you are going with three tranches, with these three companies, you will need around $10 thousand."

"Let's go for $100 thousand within 2 years."

"I don't think you need any more after the third tranche."

"It should be enough for you to retire in Thailand."

Alex felt comfortable sharing his overall thinking and how he views the investing landscape for the next few years.

CHAPTER THIRTY-FOUR

AI, Chinese AI, and Tesla: The Three Pillars

"When explaining complex concepts, anchor your words in the big picture; it's the broad strokes that often bring clarity to the intricate details." — Malcolm Gladwell

Alex paused, then thought about the big picture, careful not to get Alvin confused with the details.

He continued:

"There are three pillars that I see: AI, Chinese AI, and Tesla."

"We need to make 4x to 10x returns with AI, then gradually sell some to invest in Chinese AI, and finally, to get into their Tesla."

"That's the plan for the next two years and your roadmap to a 10x return; it's all about AI."

"Investing requires some understanding of the ups and downs."

"It can be painful, so hang in there."

"With Coinbase, my losses reached 56 percent before rebounding to 4x."

"I think at the moment, investors don't know what to think in terms of AI; they're trying to figure out if this is a bubble because the prices of AI stocks have gone up."

"Of course, this is the start of a bubble."

"It's not yet a bubble, but I think it's going to be a huge bubble."

"We just have to wait. This is the part that's not so exciting, which is good."

"You don't want to deploy all of your money into the stocks unless it's moving."

"In the meantime, if you have other investments that can keep you busy."

"But only if you know that investment is going to go up, something safe during this time."

"At the moment, I'm looking at something, but of course, it's not for everyone."

"I'm waiting on these stocks."

"I'm also waiting for another movement that's going on, this one I started about two years ago."

"Two years ago, I bought Coinbase, and since then, it has moved up about four times."

"And there's a pullback. So, I've been selling Coinbase to buy into all of these AI infrastructure plays."

"Interestingly, this April, there's an event that goes on every four years called Bitcoin Halving."

"When miners validate a blockchain, their rewards are cut in half."

"Historically, during this time, the price of bitcoin should double because the miners need to get paid, right?"

"They will not sell under cost."

"The play I'm waiting on—and it's not for everyone—is to stay with the trade until after April 20th, long enough to see the price dramatically move upward."

"For me, it's easy."

"Your part is a little bit different because you're not invested,"

"You don't have that momentum behind you."

"It's a bit scarier at $60 thousand per bitcoin."

"Bitcoin has to go up to $120 thousand to double."

"The dilemma you're facing: Sit tight with your cash because it can move when it moves, you are able to quickly commit and take advantage, right?"

"Most value investors will commit their full chunk and then forget about the market for a while, which is the best thing to do when you don't have the time to monitor."

"However, it's not the best way to get the highest return."

"You have to wait around, and while you wait, if there are opportunities, you take advantage."

"So, there is this opportunity. It's called Coinbase."

"So, if you're bored, you could take 10% from your AI campaign and invest in Coinbase when it dips."

"Once it doubles, within a few months."

"Don't get bored."

"This is just part of investing."

"Waiting is a big part."

"You don't want to overtrade."

"Each campaign lasts 2-3 years."

"Investing in AI will be faster, the time from seeding to harvesting will be 1-2 years."

"Seeding will take some time; you don't want to rush this process."

"My investment in Coinbase is approaching its end, with 2-5 months to go."

"Investing is like farming."

"The Chinese stocks are great bargains, but their AI technology is 1-2 years behind."

"The market will be very volatile in the next 6 months, a situation most people cannot handle."

"People get depressed when the price falls."

"Ups and downs will keep me busy, but it can be somewhat painful."

"Some people like their investing to be boring, and that is alright."

"It should be by design."

"I will monitor the situation, and when it is ready for you to add more seeds, I will let you know. Until then, look for those hard-to-find seeds, and happy investing."

Alex reflected on what he had shared. The analogy he used to explain how he managed investments was novel to him, but he thought it kept things interesting.

PART V -- THE INVESTOR FARMER

CHAPTER THIRTY-FIVE

Sowing the Seeds of Success: Alex's Investing Strategy

"Investing is much like farming: plant your seeds wisely, tend to your investments with patience, and harvest the rewards only after you have allowed them to grow and mature over time." — Benjamin Graham

It's Saturday on Baker Street. The place was quiet, especially the rooftop. Drake likes to have a cappuccino with his favorite cigarette to help him start the day. He looked at Alex; he knew it was going to be another challenging day for his brain. Alex likes to pack a lot into his learning sessions; today would be no exception. Nobody was around; the coffee break was short. They spoke about various topics. Alex's mind was on work. They quickly returned to the office, sitting across from each other. It felt more like an interrogation than a briefing.

Alex said, referring to a Google spreadsheet he had sent to Drake earlier, "The purpose of the spreadsheet was to help me track what and when to buy. That's how we manage money, right?"

Alex continued:

"We are like farmers, really…"

"Imagine you have different crops that represent different stocks; each grows at different rates."

"The aim is to maximize planting; we want to grow; we want

to plant the crops that yield the earliest, first."

"It's important to plan ahead, like deciding which one would grow the fastest and which one needs more attention."

"For example, we don't want to plant everything all at once, not all crops are in season at the same time. We plant at different stages."

"How do we know which are ready?" asked Drake.

Alex answered:
"We have to test; if the condition is right, it will grow."
"Put in more effort when that happens."
"We actually don't know which one will grow first, or even if it will succeed."
"But we know it will grow because we have done our research before we started the investment process."
"We have to sow different seeds—different stocks."
"Afterwards, we watch to see which one grows... which are in season with the market."

Drake asked, "How should we approach this at the beginning?"

"At the start of the investing season, the cycle could last from a few months to several years. It all starts with the initial capital. Figure out what you are interested in investing in."

"Does it matter how much money we need?"

"It's different for us because we are managing other people's money."
"Not all of the returns will go to us."
"Only a small percentage will come to us as income."
"We have to pay the bills to keep the office and the staff running."
"We need a minimum amount to make it feasible."
"However, for the vast majority of investors, the retail investor, those who invest for themselves, any amount will do."

Alex continued:

"Have a general idea of the number of stocks that will make up your farm."

"Take the capital and allocate it as a percentage, according to what you like most."

"Allocate more money to the one you think will grow the fastest."

"It doesn't have to be perfect; you can adjust later on."

"I have a lot of companies we've looked at over the years. There must be over 35 companies. Does it matter?" asked Drake.

"It depends on the amount of time you have."

"If you feel that you can keep track of the fundamentals, the people, and activists surrounding each company, then great."

"If not, cut back the number of companies until you can manage the workload."

"What is ideal to get started?"

"I think 6 is manageable."

"If you have 6 stocks, and your capital is $100 thousand, then you could start with $12k each."

"As you continue with your ongoing research, you will make adjustments later."

"Don't worry too much when you start out. Just get it done."

"How do I know which stocks to buy?"

"By doing the research, right?"

"What do you mean by research?"

Alex continued:

"Find out how the economy is doing."

"You could Google it, ask ChatGPT, or watch YouTube."

"You could even watch CNBC, Bloomberg, or Yahoo Finance."

"Ask yourself, how are people perceiving the world, and how are other investors perceiving the market?"

"The easiest way is to start by doing, by planting different seeds; you don't have to be perfect."

"You don't have to get it right the first time."

"Start with the company you are familiar with."

"This simple system is easy to learn."

"Could you give me an example?" Drake asked.

Drake seemed to follow along with what Alex wanted to do. However, he just needed real-world examples.

CHAPTER THIRTY-SIX

Planting the Seeds of Success:
Alex's Three-Tier System

"Opportunities come infrequently. When it rains gold, put out the bucket, not the thimble." — Warren Buffett

Alex continued, "Let's go back to the $12,000 for stock A; I'm going to call it Tesla."

"You need to separate that amount into three tiers; the first tier is for you to test the conditions."

"The second and third tiers are designed to increase your stack and grow your investment by building on success."

"Separating the budget for Tesla, which is $12,000, into three equal sizes of $4,000 each, is like buying in installments, only the price changes over time. I guess you want or wish the price would decrease when you are buying?"

"Well, you want the prices to go up over time, but during the buying phase, it's best that they are down."

"Let's say you sow a seed and that seed's not working out. Then what?"

"Well, then you just wait and see. From planting to when you're averaging down—it could take about one to three months per company, sometimes longer."

"That's the process of seeding."

"That is really the first tier of our three-tier system."

"Tier one, in itself, has three parts; let's call them trenches, each equally divided."

Alex went on, "My favorite is Tesla, among my other five favorite companies."

Drake interrupted:

"So I have $12,000; $4,000 is allocated evenly among the three tiers."

"The first tier is for me to average down."

"There are three parts or trenches in tier one, that makes up $1,340 per trench."

"I always start with buying the quantity that is closest to my $1,340."

"Then I would wait for the price to change over time."

"That is right," affirmed Alex.

Alex said, "If it goes down by 4 percent—what I thought would be reasonable—I would use the second trench to buy additional shares."

"When the price drops again, I would follow by buying the next trench."

"This is repeated among the other five stocks."

"After the first tier is completed, my planting-the-seed process has been completed."

"Got it, what happens when the price goes up before I could finish the three trenches?" Drake inquired.

"If the price goes up at any time during my tier one, I would stop and go directly to the second tier, skipping the remaining trenches," Alex explained.

"Going back to your analogy, tier two is about feeding the plant and allowing it to grow?" Drake confirmed.

"Yes, a lot of time is spent waiting during this stage. You have to put in more money and resources," Alex added.

Drake replied, "That is the additional 34 percent or $4,000 in your example. The amount is added by buying additional shares when I think the price is going up?"

Alex affirmed, "You must be profitable, about 4 or more percent profitable, before you add more money to your position."

"The third tier is similar; I will only add more money when I'm profitable," Drake recapped.

"Yes, can you see how you would make less when you are absolutely correct?" Alex questioned.

"However, this system will force you to be very patient with your investment money."

"Use the spreadsheet I've sent you."

"I added three areas for tier one; that's to average down, right?"

"Work on the spreadsheet according to the way you think."

"There is no right or wrong way to do it."

"Make sure it is logical to you. Make it work for you."

Drake asked, "So, I plant the seed and it's growing fast. How do I know when to harvest the profit? Worse, what if the price doesn't go up?"

"If you start planting the seed and it just takes forever, right, the price is not moving, then you know the duration is very long, so you can't afford to add more money to that seed," Alex replied.

"So, if the price goes up, then I should focus on those?" Drake sought confirmation.

"Yes, the ones you pay the most attention to," Alex responded.

"Don't worry, over time, you will start to sort it out."

"Prioritize those you can harvest the quickest, right?"

"Your profit then gets reinvested."

"You have to segment or categorize the stocks into something that grows very fast, something that grows very slow, and something in between, right?"

Alex discussed the process of buying a stock. There are many ways to do it; however, the concept is the same: make sure to ease into buying or selling. To make sure the material is clear, Alex elaborated.

CHAPTER THIRTY-SEVEN

Feeding and Harvesting

"Patience is the investor's greatest virtue, and timing their most critical skill. It is the artful pause between buying and selling that often yields the greatest profit." — Peter Lynch

Alex continued, "There are three tiers; tier one is divided into three trenches because you're not a day trader."

"So I don't expect you to be buying constantly."

"If you want to do that, it's going to mess up other routines like sleep and work."

"Just analyze each one, then place the trade and forget about it. You know it's going to be three to six months, and it will depend on many things, right?"

"That's why when you look at my spreadsheet, my ranking for the stocks always changes, like today."

"I watched a video on YouTube about Tesla's competitor, Canoo."

"They're bleeding cash and could be the next to go bankrupt."

"So, I learned something new about Tesla, that affected my view of the rank."

"So, the ranking changes constantly? The first tier is to average down. If the price drops further after I have finished allocating the money in the trenches, then what?" Drake questioned.

"You don't touch it because that's all you're willing to risk in one tier," Alex instructed.

"If you keep averaging down, you're going to run out of money for other companies."

"So, you have to follow the rule; there are only three times that you can average down."

"You have to wait for the price to go lower; if you average down too fast, too frequent."

"You cannot do that; you only have three trenches."

"You need to wait a little bit longer, right, until it becomes 10-15% down before you average down."

"Tier 2 is about feeding the plant? That is watering, fertilizing, and keeping it alive. So, it's growing nicely; then I add more money, right?" Drake sought to clarify.

"It needs to grow; that's important before you add money. If you don't see growth, then it's not working out. So wait some more," Alex explained.

"What does that mean?" Drake asked.

"That means the plant will take longer than expected to grow. You might be wrong; do more research. In the meantime, you just have to wait," Alex elaborated.

"How long should I wait?" Drake inquired.

"The whole process takes between one to two years," Alex replied.

"What's next?" Drake probed.

"Ask yourself, what's the projected price? How much money am I going to make?" Alex suggested.

"If this happens, what's the price going to be in the future?"

"A what-if pricing will keep you occupied and prevent you from overtrading."

"Try to figure out how much money you would make overall if

this or that happens."

"So, it's about keeping tabs on what could happen?" Drake concluded.

Alex continued:
"You need to check what is working, the seeds that you're planting."
"What's working, how is it so doing?"
"The seed and seeding process."

"I don't want to be overcommitted. To do this, I test the field or market; that's why I'm allocating so little money."

Alex nodded in agreement, he said, "When your investment is growing nicely,"
"There's nothing in sight that could change the outcome."
"I mean, there's no bad weather coming up, then you put in another third of the money you budgeted for that stock."

"What if there is bad news?"

"If you see something strange, or something that you don't understand, you cannot deploy the second and third tier."
"You wait and see what's going on."
Alex paused, then said, "For example, if Coinbase has a regulatory problem, you're gonna have a problem; you just need to be patient."

"Waiting is the most difficult task in investing. What do you do?"

"You will need to plant different seeds to make things interesting and profitable. If you have different stocks, you can try to predict when to start the seeding, feeding, and harvesting."

"Could you give me an example, please?"

"Yes, my second favorite company is Coinbase; I expect Coinbase to mature rapidly because I have been invested for several years now."

"That meant I've already gone through tiers 2 and 3 last year."

"This year is about harvesting then redeploying the money into the next phase of existing companies or starting a new investment cycle."

"So you need to sell Coinbase in order to redeploy the money. When do you know it's the right time to go into something new?"

"You don't really need to know how to read charts because of the way we allocate money using different tiers."

"So, you need to start seeding right after the winter (I had in mind the Crypto Winter)."

"You cannot wait too long or the condition will not be optimal."

"Too many investors will jump on opportunities if you wait too long."

"We are not talking about timing the market, more on, just do it even if you think conditions are bad."

"You are going to average down, especially in the first tier."

"Could you walk me through your thinking process with Coinbase?"

Drake seemed to grasp the strategy Alex was explaining, but needed to see its application in real-world scenarios to fully understand.

CHAPTER THIRTY-EIGHT

Harvesting the Fruits of Your Labor: Coinbase and Beyond

"In the heat of a stock market bubble, it is the cool-headed, patient strategist who not only survives but thrives, turning careful planning into profitable outcomes." — *Ray Dalio*

Alex was convinced the material could be dry. He paused and thought that perhaps he would detail his thinking.

Alex explained:

"My rationale for Coinbase..."

"I invested in Coinbase when the price was in the mid-50s."

"The price went up to the 80s, then dropped to a low in the mid-30s, so you have to be able to ride the ups and downs for this particular stock."

"Now it has gone up four times after the recent drama."

"Bitcoin halving will take place in the next few weeks; the price of bitcoin will go up by 2.2 times—based on the previous trends—from the price at the time of the event."

"We don't know the exact date and time because it will be based on the miners working on block 840,000. The price is currently at $70 thousand; that's $154 thousand per bitcoin after the halving."

"Coinbase will follow the same pattern; it's trading around $256 at the time of the halving, therefore it should be around

$563 per share."

"The increased price after the halving—in the past—took about a year to materialize. However, many are thinking this time it will take months, not a year."

"Is it a sure thing?"

"Before you go celebrating, you need to know there has always been an incident or two between the halving and the price increases."

"You will see a huge price drop; institutional traders will knock the price down and then accumulate as much inventory as possible for their future trades."

"The big money, they want to push it down before buying?" Drake asked.

"If you have that kind of buying power to move markets, wouldn't you do it as well?"

"What is the economic reasoning behind the price increase with the halving?"

Alex paused and proceeded:
"The demand will be more because of the recent ETF, but the supply is half, so the price will go up."

"That is the simple logic behind bitcoin."

"Halving means that the existing mining bitcoin reward will be reduced to half."

"This takes place every four years."

"The miners would get half of the reward."

"They have the same expense, before, if not more expense after the halving, they're not going to sell it for the same price because their income would be cut by half."

"Actually, miners would get rid of the old machines and upgrade."

"Their expenses would go up significantly."

"So they're not going to sell it for the previous price after halving; they're going to double the price so that they can make a profit, right?"

"But that is Bitcoin…"

Alex explained:
"Coinbase historically has always moved more than the bitcoin price."

"If bitcoin goes up by 10 percent, Coinbase will go up by 11 or 12 percent."

"That's why investing in Coinbase because of the halving is going to be more predictable."

"After Coinbase reaches around $500, you start to sell to take profit and relocate the money for other stocks."

"Don't abandon Coinbase because it has decades to go; it might not grow as fast as during the last few years, but it will continue to grow in the future."

"Harvest only what you need, continue to invest in Coinbase."

"So after Coinbase goes up, sell it, get the money, and start the process all over again."

"Yes, in another part of your farm, or portfolio, you might have another stock growing at a different stage; if you are like me, you are starting or would be in the middle cycle of investing in AI. Nvidia, for example, could be at the second tier; it is still going strong. This is how I view AI."

"What do you think about AI and Nvidia?"

Alex elaborated:
"I think Nvidia will be about a four-trillion-dollar company; now it's 2 trillion."

"Nvidia's price has gone up so much this last year."

"Lots of investors are scared to enter; they think it's a bubble."

"So what's happening, is it a bubble?"

Alex got excited:

"It's going to start soon, the biggest bubble of all time; it hasn't yet started."

"AI, it's all about AI for the next 2-3 years."

"There are different growth categories in AI."

"The first is going to be infrastructure, or the chip designers and makers for the data centers."

"That's why Nvidia will also double in the next year, again."

"Yes, that is how crazy this area will be."

"What do you see after that? I think this is fascinating the way you see the market."

Alex was amused; he thought and said, "Right after that, it will be SoftBank, Qualcomm, MediaTek, and AMD."

"So I think harvesting time for Nvidia will probably be in August, September of next year; that's when it should double."

"SoftBank will start; we have about 6 months to see something because it should go down and then up; that is just how the market works."

Drake was overwhelmed; he thought about the work ahead and paused before he left. Alex was happy to cover the entire process of managing the investment portfolio, especially explaining it in an analogy of farming.

PART VI

CHAPTER THIRTY-NINE

Resetting for Success: Fasting and Investing

"Fasting is Mother Nature's reset button, allowing our bodies to rejuvenate and heal in the rhythm of the natural world." — *Deepak Chopra*

Drake left and Alex got back to his reading. He spent a lot of time last year reading health books and he was convinced to be healthy one must go back to Mother Nature. He suffered from illness and depression. His body was weak and he couldn't get things in order. He tackled the problems with as much effort as he does with investing. After six months of intensive research, putting those practices to work, his health improved. He likes to tell his friends, "If you want to reclaim five years of your youth back, all you have to do is fast for ten days. Mother Nature will take that deal every time to save her own."

Jasmine narrated:
"Blue did tell me about that earlier. I do believe that. Fasting."

He doesn't understand why so many people, even those who are considerably ill, are unwilling to skip a few meals for a second chance at health. He once complained to his sister, he said:
"Did you know that it takes around 3-4 months for a person to die of starvation?"
"There is a big difference between skipping a meal versus not eating to a point where your vital organs stop functioning due to

a lack of food."

"Come on, I really don't understand."

"You don't need to be a genius to weigh the benefits of what you get and what you are asked to do, what you have to do is to give up a few meals."

"Don't eat anything, save money, the same money can be put to use for investing."

"I did tell my sister that it is very difficult for her to die from starvation."

"It's true."

Alex saw Dr. John Campbell's podcast on YouTube, he said, "Human health and economic costs of chronic disease dwarf the costs of all infectious disease in the United States by this decade's end; obesity, diabetes, and pre-diabetes are on track to debilitate 85% of American citizens. It is something to think about."

Jasmine narrated:

"Alex is so frugal, he thinks if you are not suffering due to illness, then you can save money and you have more energy to tackle your finance. I think Alex is obsessed with investing."

"Anyway..."

Alex routinely fasts, once a week on Monday. He would eat dinner on Sunday and afterward, skip a few meals until Tuesday. A friend asked him during a lunch gathering, "I cannot do that. I would die if I don't eat anything. You do intermittent fasting, right? Which meal do you have?"

"No, I only have water when I fast."

"What, you must eat something, right?"

"Just water."

"That is crazy. Don't you get hungry?" The friend asked while making an agonizing frown on her face. The expression was similar to seeing something revolting. The friend continued, "It must not be healthy, right? If I don't eat I get shaky and dizzy, I would get a headache."

"What you are describing is not because you are hungry, it is because you are going through food withdrawal. Have you ever thought that you might be addicted to food?" Alex asked.

"No, addicted to food? I don't think so. I get like that whenever I'm hungry, ever since I was a kid. I don't think so. I consider myself healthy. I'm a bit on the heavy side but who isn't around our age? We are not young anymore."

Alex was convinced after complaining to his spouse about his bloating a few days earlier, he knew it was time, he must go back to his fast. The next day he stopped eating. To his friends, he was on a hunger strike. They were determined to stop this madness.

The next day at Baker Street, Drake found a solution. He said, "The project we worked on before was not the most efficient way."

"Tell me what you have found."

"There is this online tutorial. You need to know Python. It uses NumPy, Pandas, Time Series Analysis, Python Finance Fundamentals, and Algorithmic Trading."

"That sounds interesting. How long is the course?"

"It's about 20 hours of videos."

"Alright, let's get on it."

"No, I have to replicate what you did. I'm not done."

"I'm on my own then."

After he reviewed the course, Alex thought to himself, with hesitation due to his past failures. He wasn't afraid of putting in the work, but he realized; it is never a sure thing. Nevertheless, he needs to convince himself, no matter how futile, after all, false confidence is better than none at all. He said to himself, "This is perfect, I can do it. I can fast to lose weight, clear my thoughts, and get the mental strength to tackle the monster course."

CHAPTER FORTY

Cellular Regeneration and Healing

"Fasting is not just a ritual but a biological renewal, as it prompts cellular regeneration, enhancing the body's ability to rejuvenate from within." — Dr. Mark Hyman

Alex was more determined than ever to shed the excess weight and refocused. Blue was concerned. He was pacing about when Jasmine asked, "What is the matter with you?"

"I'm worried about Alex."

"Would it help if I do some digging to see if fasting is safe?"

"Yes."

"Let me do some research on the topic. I will start with what Alex wrote."

She discovered Herbert M. Shelton, a prominent figure in the natural hygiene movement known for his writings on fasting. "He authored 'Fasting Can Save Your Life,' published mainly in the first half of the 20th century, detailing his philosophy on fasting and its health benefits."

"This book outlines Shelton's philosophy on fasting and its potential benefits for various health conditions." She explained. "Alex drew inspiration from this book."

Alex also wrote to his friends:

'I fast from Sunday dinner to Tuesday lunch, and sometimes until dinner, that's 40 or 45 hours per week.'

'I've found that fasting is not so straightforward.'

'Overeating before the fast takes longer to get the healing

effect.'

'If I'm not uncomfortable or feeling pain, I'm not healing.'

'It's really, no pain, no gains.'

'So, the pre-fast diet influences the fasting experience.'

'Consider the impact of drinking coffee during the fast.' He wrote.

'Coffee doesn't seem to completely halt the fasting process, it is not ideal due to its impact but it doesn't halt the process.'

'Interesting, right?'

'The healing begins when digestion ceases, but not entirely.'

'I'm going with that for now.'

'What you consume before beginning the fast is important.'

'It appears, digestion and healing, often seen as mutually exclusive, may not be so.'

'I don't have any evidence that supports that; it's only a feeling.'

'I think our body is smart; the digestive and healing processes are complex and likely not just an on/off switch.'

'Fasting helps restore balance within the body, promoting good microorganism growth, which aids in pre-digestion.'

'Fasting should last as long as you need to clear your gut, reduce stored fat, and ensure the healing of existing diseased body parts is completely halted.'

'And reversed. That is important...'

'This is the physical aspect of fasting.'

'There is this whole other layer that involves our mental state...'

'Let's not get into that.'

'The brief of it is.'

'You have to feel good, manage your dopamine release, and manifest a positive mood to create the frequency your body naturally vibrates at.'

'Everything is about frequency, the universe vibrates.'

'Our mind must be healthy before our body can be.'

Alex's advice was to, 'have a wonderful relationship with food,' as a prerequisite to living a healthy life.

Jasmine said:

"Shelton's book emphasizes that fasting is a natural instinct among animals."

"The book cited many examples."

"I don't think you need to worry, Blue."

"It seems Alex has thoroughly researched this topic."

"I have records spanning almost 2 years."

Blue said, "Thanks, Jas. I don't understand humans. Maybe I don't understand nature also. I cannot fast. I'm always hungry. Wait, I think you are right, cats don't eat when we are sick or injured." He paused and left as quietly as he came. It was time to see if Alex was making progress with the cryptocurrency.

CHAPTER FORTY-ONE
Deciphering the Crypto Code

"In every asset lies a fundamental value, often obscured beneath layers of market sentiment. Through diligent analysis, we uncover these hidden gems, revealing their true worth." — Warren Buffett

Alex was busy working on the analysis for cryptocurrencies when Blue approached. He revisited the points he had mentioned to Drake earlier. He didn't involve Jasmine; instead, he had a chat with Gemini and directly consulted OpenAI's Chat. After going back and forth for about an hour, he was pleased with the list:

"Increase and maintain a high number of small wallets."

"Analyze transaction volume, types, and average costs to gauge usage patterns and network health."

"Ensure decentralization of nodes."

"Monitor code commit frequency and volume in project repositories."

"Identify the number and type of key integrations with the project, such as exchanges, wallets, and DeFi platforms."

"Track code contribution frequency, volume, and contributors to repositories."

"Evaluate the team and advisors by their number, reputation, relevant experience, and community engagement."

"Inquire about the quantity of external funders, funding amounts, and funding structures."

"Jasmine, what do you think about my list?" asked Alex.

"I have analyzed the readability of the content, and it would be difficult for most people to understand."

"Can you help me analyze it and recommend a way to explain it better?"

"Sure. Primarily, we need to ensure the user base for the digital 'wallets'—akin to online bank accounts—is expanding, which would signify active and increasing transactions, as well as a growing code base. The project needs to achieve meaningful adoption across diverse user groups. The network must be decentralized, which is key. Equally important is the involvement of reputable team members, external advisors, and active community participation."

"Can you explain it even simpler?"

"Alright, think of it this way," said Jasmine, "We're creating our very own startup, like a mini-company, and we're building this super cool app."

"So, first off, we need lots of people to download and use our app."

"And we don't want just any users; we want all sorts of people to join in. This way, our app gets all kinds of cool ideas and feedback, making it even better!"

"Our app works better when everyone gets a say, where everyone's ideas matter."

"We need smart people who know how to make apps, plus some wise advisors who've been in the business longer than us, giving us pro tips."

"When we look at crypto projects, we have to view them from these perspectives."

Alex said, "Great, this will give us the 'what' we need to do. Later we will need to figure out the 'how'. I don't have time to do it now. Can you remind me please?"

"Yes, I will add that to your schedule."

Now, Alex realized that Blue was still around and turned his attention to his friend. However, he has to check in on Helen first. She was visually different.

CHAPTER FORTY-TWO
The Shadow of Uncertainty

"Innovation has the power to reshape the landscape of inequality, but as it propels us forward, it also casts a shadow of uncertainty over the future, challenging us to navigate the unknown with wisdom and foresight." — Elon Musk

Helen is liked by everyone in her class. She is considerate to a fault. Alex asked, "Why are you still friends with her? Didn't she bully you?"

"No, Daddy, she was upset with me. Anyway, it wasn't her. It was another girl. She sided with the other girl."

"Still, if she bullied you before... You don't need to be friends with everyone."

"Oh, Daddy, it's okay now."

Alex was working on a project over the weekend; it was about OpenAI, from there he explored open-source AI. The weekend project became a little more, down the rabbit hole he went. Alex said, "Wow, I cannot believe this. I don't have to hire anyone to do marketing."

"Blue, I think I cannot fully get this to work because I'm not good enough. I'm sure if I spend a little more time, it would be possible. Sorry I haven't had time for you earlier."

He was working on a project called AutoGPT, the autonomous agent, where, just with a few lines of code, he could assign tasks like research and development. The software, on its own, then would go about the business of getting the task done, autonomously. Alex had been dabbling with coding; his work got him involved in different parts of the process, some were more technical than others. After a while, he knew enough to get started but not to complete projects on his own. Coding was never his expertise domain; however, without resources, he was it.

"Blue, I think I'm in trouble. Who is going to be hiring an old man like me? Look at what is happening. After a few weeks, I got this thing to research and write reports. I got this to work and I don't need to hire anyone." Alex continued to complain to Blue:

"The code is so buggy."

"I got it to work and then after a few updates, it doesn't work anymore."

"I know it's community-driven and it is free, but still."

"It will get better and fast."

"I don't know what my kids are going to do."

"I'm not sure how they are going to adapt to this environment where AI will be doing a lot of the work that humans are doing now?"

"I'm sure they will be fine."

"They are not like me."

"My kids are born in the digital age, born into this technology."

"They can do things that I cannot."

Alex realized that he was talking to Blue again, this time strangely Blue was not talking back. Perhaps Blue never did. I guess you don't have to talk when I'm doing all the talking.

Alex continued, "We live in a world where the rich get richer and the poor are left without much."

"The problem is not limited to resources; it is because some of us have too much and others don't have enough."

"Think about it, what happens when companies are able to hire fewer people to do the same work, only doing it much better?"

"I know you are just a cat."

"What happens to people who are displaced?" Alex was in his usual pondering state, questioning everything.

"Companies don't exist without customers."

"If they are not paying people to do the work, then people cannot buy."

Alex pondered and said, "I think if you live in a capitalist system, a system that is based on greed."

"Being greedy is not a good thing for society."

"A system of obsolescence, where things are built not to last."

"Where governments need people to buy, to spur on the economy."

"It is a system where if you stop doing, like a shark, you have to swim and go forward, if you don't, you sink."

"This is a system where corporations own everything."

"In a capitalist system, you have to participate or die, financially."

"I'm going to have to teach my kids to invest so that they can better prepare themselves for this new world."

"I don't have much time."

"The problem is not because I start and stop projects due to a lack of interest. I stop mainly because the projects were obsolete. Every few weeks a new open-source project would come along and replace what I did the prior weeks."

"What do I expect, this is the age of disruption."

"It is better if I don't do anything and wait for the latest and greatest, once the dust settles."

"Come to think about it, how much runway do I have? I only have months until someone overtakes me; I don't have years."

"I need to make progress. I have people relying on me."

"If I'm going to be successful, I've got to hurry up and work on it."

"Let me come up with a list of what I need to do."

"The first thing is to create a token and raise money. That is the fastest..."

Alex paused, "Thanks for listening, Blue. You are a great cat."

CHAPTER FORTY-THREE

Helen's Lesson in Social Awareness

"Youth often stumbles upon its power by accident, finding in acts as simple as a boycott, the profound force of unity. Even those deemed powerless can wield great influence when they stand together." — *Malala Yousafzai*

After he vented to Blue, Alex was convinced that Helen had to learn the ropes. Alex has been eagerly anticipating the revival of the crypto market. During the past four years, the industry has undergone a metamorphosis of its own, transforming from the Wild West. Politicians are being paid, sorry, being lobbied, and people in the crypto industry are slowly evolving. It is still early; the last period right after the 'Crypto Winter' made a lot of people rich investors in the past.

He was thinking about how to get Helen to help with the research as well. The research would be perfect to get her started. They were walking to the train, Helen asked, "So are we still boycotting?"

"Yes, we are boycotting. One of the companies we are boycotting came out and said that due to a misunderstanding, that was the reason their income will be affected. You have to read between the lines, they didn't say they didn't support the war, instead, it was due to misunderstanding. The boycott is working."

"So, who do we support?" Helen was asking her dad because she just wanted a conversation. Alex thought it was a wonderful teaching opportunity.

"We support small and local businesses where they pay a living wage to their employees."

"Do we support the train stations?"

"No, do you know what is going on? Politicians take money from people and build these stations, then they give it to businesses that then turn around and make money from the same people. They have a fancy name, they like to call it privatization, it is criminal. No, we support small and local businesses."

Helen said, "Ok, Daddy. I'm going now, bye, I love you." Helen was particularly happy this morning, thought Alex. What Alex didn't know was that Blue and Jasmine were now buddies. Helen's new curiosity was about Blue hanging around the table as an odd thing when he prefers the kitchen more. She was determined to get to the bottom.

CHAPTER FORTY-FOUR

The Secret's Out

"Youth often stumbles upon its power by accident, finding in acts as simple as a boycott, the profound force of unity. Even those deemed powerless can wield great influence when they stand together." — *Malala Yousafzai*

Helen made sure no one else was in the office but Blue. She quietly walked up, "Hey."

"Meow."

"What, that was weird, I thought you were talking to Jasmine."

"Wait, Helen, he could only talk to me."

She was thinking when she said, "I wonder if I can change that. Let me debug my translator so that Blue and I can speak in his native tongue. Then he could talk to you in human tongue."

"What, wait."

Jasmine then told Helen everything about Blue, about how he spoke to Alex, how he stopped...

Blue was speechless.

"There, I think I got it," said Jasmine.

"Meow," said Blue.

"Great, I can understand you now. Don't use human tongue to talk to me anymore. I know you are reluctant, but Helen promised not to tell anyone about you."

"Meow, meow," said Blue, reluctantly.

After a few days passed, Helen was able to understand Blue. Helen was overwhelmed, "Blue, it's true, you can talk."

"Helen, you have to keep your promise, or I will stop talking to you. My dear child, you cannot tell anyone," Blue was worried.

"I promise. Now don't worry. I have to go to school. Daddy is waiting. I will not tell him. It is our secret."

"Don't worry, she is a big girl, and she will keep her promise. I know things about humans. About this human. Since her dad wrote a lot of entries about her," said Jasmine.

Blue said nothing and dashed off.

Jasmine narrated:

"That was tense. Let's check up on Alex."

Alex was thinking about leaving Singapore again. To Alex, Singapore was very expensive but safe. Every now and then, he would call his relatives in the States or friends overseas to ask what life was like there. The answers were never very promising. Sure, occasionally he thought about moving to Vietnam or elsewhere, where things were cheaper, where life was a little bit slower. Alex's thoughts were his way of escaping.

After dinner, Alex said, "What do you think about Anne's situation, Helen?"

"Bad."

"What do you mean?"

"I mean, she doesn't have any money. Sure, Bill works, but she has to rely on him. That's not good."

"Maybe we can help her. Anne doesn't like to invest because she said it's boring. This could be an opportunity, since I want to teach you about investing. We could do both. We feed Anne our updates after we've gone over them together."

"Wait, are we going to teach people how to invest?"

"No, it is just for entertainment and something we can do together. It's really my way, a more constructive outlet for me to let off some steam. Besides, you have read and edited my book, and I thought it would be a great way to put it into practice."

"It's not entertainment, it's work. You mean, people are not going to take what we do as something real?"

"No, it will be fiction."

"Wait, that's really confusing."

"What do you mean it's confusing? We are just going to write fiction on investing?"

"So, Blue is still our cat?"

"You and I will be ourselves?"

"Drake is the uncle who came a few days ago."

"Sifu is still Sifu." Helen is fond of him now that she is older. She was scared of him when she was younger and took his class.

"You are also the editor, so you have two roles, OK Helen? Wait, that is not all, you will have to be the main protagonist. The Holmes version of our story, the detective."

"Sure, Daddy. I'm going to do my work."

"So, I'm going to study. I will start at 10 am until 2 pm," said Helen. She was delighted but not excited. She was ten years old and living in Singapore. Alex said to her one day in his usual speech to motivate her, "You live in Singapore, so you are not a kid. Why? There are no kids living in Singapore. There are just students. Once you are born in Singapore, you were a baby, then a toddler, then a student. No kids." As he said out loud, it was correct but felt betrayed by what he knew and heard.

He would often quote Sir Robinson, the famed keynote speaker on Ted Talk. Robinson said, "Formal school kills creativity." Alex held onto Robinson's message that children and education are not a one-size-fits-all. However, Alex felt powerless to do anything about it in Singapore.

He secretly wished the government would ban all tuition in Singapore, similar to what China did, decisively, last year. Education is now an arms race, thought Alex. There are no clear winners in such a race where children are robbed of their youth. It puts parents in a strange dilemma of having to rationalize the good of torturing their own on a promise of giving them a better future. As if there is any good coming out of wars. This was no different, a war to see which child will be better equipped to live life in the future, more realistically which child is willing to put aside the joy of living now... It is a pure waste of talent and creative energy.

CHAPTER FORTY-FIVE

Every Little Bit Matters: Alex's Investment Advice

> *"Compound interest is the eighth wonder of the world. He who understands it, earns it; he who doesn't, pays it." — Albert Einstein*

He quickly snapped out of his yet another depressing thought.

"How was your class?" Alex asked Helen.

"It was alright." She didn't look particularly happy.

"Tell me more?" Alex knew it was like squeezing for the last few drops of lemon. He should have stopped but didn't.

"I have to talk to you about something."

"The other day I saw you were buying candies and not eating them."

"Instead, you gave them to your friends."

"The thing was, nobody wanted it."

"I think we have to talk about value," Alex said. Helen protested at first.

However, she realized that he couldn't be stopped once he got started. She was looking for a way out of another long talk.

Alex said:

"I want you to be a good investor."

"You have to save money so you can invest."

"Instead of ordering a main course, appetizer, and a drink."

"Just order what you need, order only what you can eat."

"Don't worry about what other people are having."

"If you are not hungry and the waiter, all of your friends are waiting for you, what do you do?"

"I'll tell them I'm not hungry."

"You don't have to eat when you are not hungry."

"I think it is unhealthy and wasteful to eat if you are still full."

"Eat if you are hungry and enjoy it. Just don't overdo it."

"The other day I was out with a friend and he was having a buffet and I was surprised he ordered another main dish on top of the buffet."

"The extra dish cost $25 more."

"The money wasn't important to him."

"It was about enjoying a meal with friends."

"Sure, I understand that."

"I'm sure if the waiter said they were out of steak, it wouldn't have affected him much."

"The waiter was glad for the order."

"Still, he didn't need it. It was wasteful."

"If you go to ChatGPT or Bard and ask it to calculate what that $25 cost over 30 years, invested at 20 percent returns."

"I did that, and do you know what I got back?"

"What?" Helen asked.

Alex explained:

"Almost $6 thousand, that was for 30 years; that same amount would be $59 thousand for 40 years."

"Everything matters; every little amount that you spend, when you add it up, matters."

"I've heard people tell me when I talk to them about investing, they told me they had no money."

"As I'm talking to them, they would pull out their cigarettes."

"Cigarettes are not cheap, you know. If you add up all the little things that you don't need, especially bad habits, you can definitely invest."

"Those bad habits will rob you of the joy in life."

"People tell me that's their enjoyment."

"Sure, I get it, it's enjoyment until the health is gone and misery comes."

"If you ask me, don't waste money like that, use it, let money make a living for you."

"How was your polliwog?" Alex changed the subject. He was preaching, and he knew it.

"There was only one left."

"What happened?"

"I brought it to my science teacher."

"It turns out you have to feed it. It can only survive without food for two days."

"Did your friend bring food for them?"

"Yes, but it was too late." Helen was sad but had accepted the facts; she had killed so many polliwogs.

"Oh." Alex didn't know what else to say. He wanted to scold her but refrained. A few days before, Helen jumped into a ditch and captured a handful of polliwogs for her school science project.

Helen went to bed, and Alex did a quick search for Coinbase, got an update on the price. Sighed. The stock has gone up $122 a share in the past year; by anyone's measurement, it's a huge success. Alex was different; he believed in the certainty of things. There are so many uncertainties. His friends, on occasion, would send him links to YouTube videos on investing and would ask him to comment on their validity. Recently, many of the posts were of the doom and gloom nature. He couldn't stand it because he knew how difficult it was to shield himself from external influences. However, this time he had to make an exception; his friend just came back from her trip to China, luckily for him, she and a bunch of friends were having dinner the next day.

CHAPTER FORTY-SIX

A Glimpse into China

"Nothing surpasses the deep understanding gained from setting foot in a country yourself. To truly grasp what's going on, you must breathe its air, walk its streets, and speak to its people." — Anthony Bourdain

"I ditched my husband and went with a friend," Binni was visiting Shanghai, the economic commerce of China, with her family. She pulled out her phone and showed us a picture of the Peace Hotel, "Fairmont," the iconic luxury hotel. Outside, it looks like an old building one could easily mistake, as one of the buildings in Manhattan. Inside was a different matter with its high vaulted ceiling. Immediately, your eyes are drawn to the huge chandeliers and cathedral-like arch with intricate moldings on the sides. Towards its sides, the stately grandeur white walls, then down at the floor, it's covered with exquisite Persian rugs.

A slew of people walked up to the menu posted outside near the entrance, one by one they gazed at it and then retreated to a more comfortable distance. The impenetrable shield that was so effective, the sign might have said, 'Do not enter if you don't have money.' Binni said, one by one, "the people in front would walk up to the menu, look at it, and leave."

Jasmine narrated:
It was the most effective self-imposed restriction that could have said, no entrance to the poor. The only decency was that

people don't mind. Society has routinely beaten us down that collectively the weight of our self-worth is a fraction of what it once was. In youth, we were invincible, now in adulthood, we are a shadow of ourselves, we call that reality.

As if the price tag was not enough of a deterrent, she walked to the door and was greeted right away by the staff, who spoke in Chinese, "Where are you going?"

She proudly replied, "The cafe," and pointed a route to the table. Binni sat, the menu came, she ordered and was determined not to notice the price. "I had a small cake and two coffees. It cost $70."

"What, let me get you the whole cake," Alex and Binni were dining at the Trade Wind at the American Club in Singapore. She smiled. They both knew it wasn't the same.

"Every year in December I have been visiting China. This year it was very bad. The streets were empty. I went to the EV Show, it was empty." Binni swiped her phone and showed a picture of a car, "She continued, "This sports car is only $70 thousand, it's so cheap." A friend sitting across from the table interrupted, "It's only expensive in Singapore."

Alex wanted to get the scoop so he sat closer to Binni. She said, "You should just go and take some pictures. Things are bad, very bad over there."

Alex asked, "last year, 2023, was a year of opposites, what I thought was true turned out to be very different. I've heard two sides of the story in China, there are people who said that China is doing well and another group is saying that China is in bad shape."

"Yes, people are buying, people are still buying food, small ticket items, not the big stuff, people have to eat, a five renminbi meal, that is $1, it's cheap and people are buying," replied Binni.

"What you don't see, people are not buying cars, they are not buying properties, the big ticket items. There are half finished buildings 10 minutes' drive from the smaller cities in China where they build the first and second story and just left it unfinished, these are not cities, the buildings in the ghost cities are different, at least they are finished, these buildings are worse, only the first and second story are done. Things are very bad."

"What do you think is in store for 2024?"

"I think the market is going to go up at the beginning of this year, but by March, however, it will go back down."

"What do you mean? I've heard a lot from different gurus, they mostly said the economy is going to go down."

"Not at the beginning of the year, I look at the copper to gold ratio, when compared this way, historically copper is a good indication of the economy."

Binni wasn't justifying, nor did she have to, she said calmly and as factual as self-evident. "Right now, China stocks are cheap, but nobody's buying. I think things will get worse."

"What do you think will happen?"

"China will have to come up with a stimulus. They are going to cut the deposit rates. This will make people put their money elsewhere, not in the banks, to find higher interest. This will stimulate the economy."

"There is the financial economy and the real economy, which one?"

"I'm not sure, the Politburo will decide."

"What? Do you mean the CCP?"

"No, the CCP is made up of a lot of people

, there are only seven people in the Politburo. They decide

what to do in terms of stimulating the economy."

"I have been looking at the China stocks and you are right. I thought they are cheap. Alibaba, Tencent, JD."

"JD.com?" Interjected Binni.

"I am going to start accumulating positions in China stocks." What Alex meant to say, but didn't, was that he will start a position in the small funds he manages for his family. He is well aware of his financial situation. Reflecting on his circumstances, unlike Binni, 2023 was the year when his grocery bills were surgically cut. No more organic apples, instead an apple was good enough. The budget was precise. All unnecessary items were removed, going to the cinema was a thing of the past. Simple pleasures were then just an ice cream at McDonald's. Sadly, the family was boycotting the war. Helen said, "We cannot eat at McDonald's." Alex will need to explain the family's position.

CHAPTER FORTY-SEVEN

Investing in Change

"If you're going through hell, keep going." — Winston Churchill

Back at Baker Street, Alex thought about what Helen said. He paused, he didn't believe in the reality of the war. He called Anne and spoke about the war, Alex said:

"Technically, you cannot have a war where one side is the occupation force. It's resistance."

"The poor will always be bullied in this world."

Anne asked, "Why are you protesting?"

"I was really depressed."

"A few months back I took a break from writing. I just wanted to understand the complexity of the situation."

Anne questioned:

"Why would you do that?"

"You know our democracy is in turmoil."

"You need to support the free press."

"That is the most important cause that you can tackle."

Alex rebutted:

"Well, I think there are many other things that are important."

"We have the 'Free Press' in the States."

They both knew that you can say what you want but it will

cost you.

Anne said:

"No we don't."

"You should not be so out there."

"I've been reading about your posts."

"People can pull strings and make things hard for you and your family."

"I just want to give you a heads up."

"Just do your work and live out our lives, we are not young anymore."

Alex explained:

"I'm alright now, I was depressed."

"Besides, those posts were not written by me. Also, the stories were about what other people, experts in the area."

"These are important topics that we must talk about."

"We all need to have these dialogs."

"Anyway..."

"I have given myself permission to be ok, I've resolved to contribute what I could."

"I have divested all of my investments in companies, those that supported the war."

"I will personally not buy anymore; ice cream is out."

What Alex didn't say but many of the companies were partly owned by his icon, the famed investor that everyone knows. Alex had spent the majority of his twenties, thirties, and part of his forties in admiration of this man who he thought was brilliant. His mind and the uncommon investment routine he had. Alex thought his success was due to his ability to manage his schedule, his routine. He was sad and secretly wished that investor would get on the phone with the CEOs and give them a nudge to get out of the situation so he can take the kids for ice cream again.

Jasmine said, "That is not going to happen. That investor

doesn't micro-manage. He spent the better part of his life making money and he has entrusted his wealth to a man who has now been revealed as a closet monster to society."

Later that afternoon, Alex and Helen were walking with his brother. Alex thought, even the greatest of the great do, on occasion, make bad judgment. In the last two decades, Alex's investing principles have steadily been moving away from the old.

They were talking about investing. Alex said, "I was in between Graham and Buffett. I'm now more towards Livermore and Wyckoff." Alex now thinks "Value Trading" is suitable and it's a more descriptive name for what he was working on. The phrase has grown on him during the past few months.

Alex tends to repeat himself with the same messages to different people. It is his way of solidifying and making what he was thinking at the time, to be more real, more concrete. The other reason was he was obsessed with the idea and could not keep himself away from the subject.

Alex said:
"Last year, I was depressed."
"I started a paper trading..."
"...Livermore was a force of nature."
"His odd habit was to celebrate the new year by locking himself in the Chase bank vault, in solitary, where he could go over his trades for the year..."
Alex repeated what he said to Drake earlier. "I've spent three months trading and made $60 million..."
"...The challenge is to start with a small amount, just $10 to $20 thousand..."

Alex knew it was almost impossible but he believed in accountability so it was imperative for him to put his intention out there, out in the universe, that if another soul knows of his goal, it would somehow be more diligent in his efforts and his actions. His brother didn't really care much for trading, Alex knew that; he was trying to work out the details in his head and he found that often when he talks about it, the idea will crystallize into something more tangible. Alex knew that if he succeeds, he needed to have a way where his sister could mirror his trading. He thought, bringing him back to the app. Jasmine said, "I guess I have to come up with a plan. I will get Blue and Helen to help."

Meanwhile, Alex needs to book another trip, this time he found himself frustrated not knowing if he was dealing with a person or a bot.

CHAPTER FORTY-EIGHT

A Vegetarian's Plight

"Risk comes from not knowing what you're doing."
— Warren Buffett

Alex was agitated after spending 30 minutes on a chat with a person or bot on the Trip app. The agent wrote,

"I will submit your request after you check in."

"Wait, that doesn't make sense. I can check in 2 hours before the flight. I need to do the meal request anywhere between 2-3 days in advance, don't I?"

"I can submit a request, but there is no guarantee."

"I'm vegetarian and have been for almost 20 years," Alex was visibly concerned. He could fast during the trip. However, he was thinking about who owns the company. Meal selection cannot be so difficult. If there is a thread to pull, this would be it. He thought this could be a short-selling opportunity. He wondered if there was something else wrong with the business model. The agent is obviously following procedures, or is she? Who came up with the process, he thought to himself while waiting. He was aware he was being agitated. He remembered David Sedaris' advice, turn bad experiences into a writing opportunity; in Alex's case, turn it into trading op-

portunities. Maybe this is a rogue agent, overzealous in disclaimers who is not following protocols, or something else?

"I've submitted your request to the airline, but I cannot guarantee there won't be a charge. If there is a charge, you will need to pay for it."

"No, I won't pay again for something I've already paid."

"I understand."

"Thank you."

"What meals would you like?"

Alex was perplexed, this was mentioned before.

"Wait, are you a person or a bot?"

"I'm a person."

"Vegetarian, thank you for helping," Alex was confused; he thought to himself, I cannot be the first vegetarian to use their service.

"I've submitted your request to the airline, but I cannot guarantee there won't be a charge. If there is a charge, you will need to pay for it."

"Again, I'm not paying for meal selection. That is crazy; you don't go to a cafe, pay for a meal, then pay again to select your meal. I cannot eat meat."

"I understand."

"Your job is difficult. I cannot imagine why your company has this process."

"Can you confirm?"

"Yes, for the vegetarian meals."

Again, the same message came up.

"I've submitted your request to the airline, but I cannot guarantee there won't be a charge. If there is a charge, you will need to pay for it."

"There are no guarantees in life but death; I don't need to be reminded that I have no guarantees today that I will not die. I can confirm that I'm a vegetarian."

"It is just a disclaimer."

"I shouldn't need legal representation on this chat."

"I have submitted your request to the airline."

"Thank you."

He thought about it, added a note to himself, "pull thread, Trip." A few hours later, he received an email that read, "The optional service you applied for has been confirmed. We hope you enjoy your trip." He pulled the note from the drawer, crossed off the task, and wrote, "maybe it's a buying opportunity." He thought about the bad experience and decided not to do anything.

He later spoke to Anne about it. Alex was sitting and staring at his screen, not doing anything. Alex thought it would be a wonderful learning experience. This is how he got to know about things that are often not on most investors' radars. He called Anne.

"What did you do after the chat?" Anne asked. Alex was upset about the incident, enough to mention it but not enough to do anything about it. His excuse was a good learning opportunity, but in reality, it was partially venting.

"I decided not to do anything."

"What if you didn't get the email?"

"Then I thought there might have been an opportunity to see what else is wrong with the company. At the moment, the process is odd, and I will not buy from them again, but it is not enough for non-vegetarians to not do business with them. It's like going to a restaurant that doesn't cater to vegetarians. It doesn't make sense, but this world doesn't have to make sense to everyone; it only has to make sense to the majority. I find that lots of businesses leave too many low-hanging fruits, simply because they don't have enough oversight; there is no one responsible for new business."

"How about buying the stocks?"

"I wouldn't at this point because they are not exceptional.

If they are bad, then there might be grounds for shorting the stocks."

"I hear you."

"I don't want to do the research unless they are great at something."

After the complaint, he went back to work.

Alex's attention is increasingly turned to the war, both in Ukraine and Palestine, more so with the latter. There are talks of escalation.

PART VII

CHAPTER FORTY-NINE

Taking a Stand: Seva's Plan for Change

"It is in your hands to create a better world for all who live in it." — *Nelson Mandela*

Alex was right, and more of his inner circles are beginning to talk about the war, again. At Baker Street, Seva visited.

"BDS doesn't go far enough; in 2024, we are going to weaponize divestment," said Seva.

"This morning I was upset about a chat I was on. So, I like where you are going with this. I have to tell you. You are lucky that you are not in the US. I would not know anything about it. There is a media stranglehold on what people can write and say," replied Alex.

"I don't think so. You can say and write what you want, but you will pay for it. Everything has a cost."

"Tell me, what do you have in mind, specifically? Do you seriously think that everyday people like us have a say in democracy? I know collectively we do, but..." Alex paused, looking out the window and glancing down at the street. He saw a familiar lady walking along with a young boy. The pair walked with springs under their feet, gravitating their every step effortlessly. He wondered if that was what joy looks like. For the last several years, he has been fighting a long battle to keep the business afloat. Recovering from failure takes longer than expected; his mind still has flashbacks to the past.

Jasmine narrated, "Our friend Alex is depressed. I'm not going to tell Helen that."

"Are you thinking of mobilizing the political base and getting voters to pay attention to what is happening in the world, instead of pointlessly trying to make their lives bearable?" asked Alex.

"These ideas are about working within the political system," said Seva.

"No, for that to work, it requires sensible people who care about people to do something; these are often the same people who are being paid to look the other way, to close one eye."

"My argument is that you have to work outside of that system," Seva continued.

"I saw a video, the host said, 'Israel spends 70m,' to silence the majority of Americans."

"I don't think that is accurate," Alex replied.

"Each election cycle, politicians spend billions."

"It is a crazy democracy process that goes on every few years."

"Israel cannot silence Americans."

"We are simply too busy with our broken dreams and broken relationships, kept distracted and brainwashed to believe that it is taboo to speak about politics and religion."

"Do you know why? If the average person doesn't pay attention, the people in charge can get away with murder."

"That is strong language. It's a war, right?" Alex asked.

"No, it's not a war," Seva replied.

"What is the plan?"

Seva unveiled her plan: "Create a fund, an actively managed fund."

"Look, bad people will always lose."

"The fund will start positions in these companies which for some reason the shareholders are asleep at the wheel."

"The CEO and management team think ethics and morality are not important."

"We have to gently remind these arrogant assholes who are in charge."

"If the soft approach doesn't work, then we get nasty."

"It is also in our interest to clean up the scum who are in charge of the corporate world as it is our duty to hold politicians accountable."

"The hard approach is slowly to take a large position in the bad actor and shake up the management from the inside if they are cheap; if they are at a premium, then we back their competitors, let's take their lunch money for bullying mankind."

"Why are you so worked up? It's a rhetorical question; don't worry about it. I've changed my mind; I don't like where this is going. You are really picking a fight. How are you going to win? Come on, Seva, these are the business elites; you very well know who runs the country. It's not the politicians; it's not the voters. Do I really have to tell you?" Alex insisted.

"No, stop reminding me, Uncle," said Seva.

Seva was visibly upset at the situation. She needed to cool down. They said their goodbyes and dashed off as quickly as she came.

Jasmine, Blue, and Helen huddled the next morning. Jasmine said, "Did you notice Seva yesterday?"

"Let's not go crazy. We already have a lot of work ahead. We still have to help Steve; with so much to do, I'm not sure that it is even possible," replied Jasmine.

"There are so many companies to look at," said Helen.

"Not to mention, there are thousands more cryptos too," she added.

"What happened to Seva?" Helen asked.

"That is not such a crazy idea; look, if we are going to help people. This might be a way to right what is wrong and help people make money as well," said Helen.

Blue was confused.

"We could create a crypto DeFi fund, create synthetics of assets. I've found a lot of documentation on Alex's computer relating to his previous project," Jasmine explained. "Alright, you have to tell us more. I will talk to Seva. I don't want Daddy to worry about this. He has too many things on his mind."

"Meow, I agree," said Blue.

"Also, I have to look into the property market; there are rumors of Blackstone defaulting. The China economy is on the brink of collapse."

"Yes, you look into those and tell us what you know," said Helen.

Jasmine was curious and wanted to find more information on Seva and how Alex met her.

CHAPTER FIFTY

Seva's Bold New Concept

"All truth passes through three stages. First, it is ridiculed. Second, it is violently opposed. Third, it is accepted as being self-evident." — Arthur Schopenhauer

Seva and Alex worked together on a charity first responder project called Seva Corps. The idea was to create an army of volunteers in every country with the goal of funding humanitarian aid within hours of any disaster, globally, and to mobilize the corps from the bottom up. Local volunteers would gather the funds and pay for necessities, while international funds would be transferred through their own network, built on blockchain infrastructure. Despite their hard work, the project didn't take off. Banks didn't like the idea, so they couldn't create bank accounts in key countries, and governments only saw how their network could sidestep regulatory processes. Eventually, Seva had to stop working on the project.

Seva was a petite Latina from Los Angeles, smart and in her late twenties. She could have chosen any university but selected Berkeley because her boyfriend was there first. Knowing she wanted a family, they got married after college. Her husband writes fiction. Coming from a wealthy background, her father was a prominent commodities trader who retired in his early forties and managed a small farm just north of Stockton. He created a sizable trust fund for her and her siblings. As the youngest of three, Seva credited her independence to her birth order, saying, "Mom and Dad got too tired of micromanaging my brother and sister's lives; by the time I came around, they didn't have the energy, so I was free to do what I wanted." With the financial freedom to travel, she chose Singapore for its safety for kids and the absence of capital gains tax. The young family didn't need to work for a living. Alex mentored Seva in her investments.

Seva called and said, "Uncle, I think you're making it too complicated."

"What do you mean?" Alex asked.

"Well, you're overthinking it."

"I don't understand what you mean."

"I need your help to discuss how it would work." After weeks of procrastination, he decided to get help from his friend. "What do you think I should do?" Alex asked.

"Yeah, I think your investing and entertainment apps, the two apps, would have an intersection where the two circles overlap," Seva gestured with her hands.

Alex said:
"I'm not sure.
Now that you've said it out loud, I just can't see how an investment app could be part of the music app.
If we go back to the core, to what makes the music app unique and so necessary, there are just two core features, right?
There's the radio mode and the on-demand mode.
I don't like that description, 'on-demand,' but it's easy to understand. Maybe 'jive' mode would be better.
Anyway, how do we combine these two with investing?"

"At that point, what you're talking about is something like an NFT, where you have a group of people owning the rights to the music, a group thing," Seva continued, and Alex, though impatient, listened without interrupting.

Seva loved the idea of the Rabbit device.

"No, I don't see your project as an app," she continued, "what was cool about the Rabbit was the concept that an app should be a thing of the past."

Seva was convinced:

"Why do we need an app for this and an app for that?

I always thought that didn't make sense until someone articulated it.

So, it shouldn't be an app.

I was thinking, as you have, that where the two circles intersect and overlap is where we should find a common ground for the new app.

You cannot build two apps. I couldn't come up with anything that makes sense.

I'm beginning to think that instead of narrowing the focus, we have to make it even bigger, have a bigger circle that would encompass both investing and music."

"What do you mean?" Alex asked.

Seva continued:

"Like a social media platform, only it's not an app.

I think the concept of an app is now outdated and it was made clear.

That thought was out, and the world is vibrating on that idea; everything exists as a frequency, soon everyone will embrace the nonsense of being captured by a screen," Seva, who was into meditation and healing through positive thinking, added, "That is going to change. So, it cannot be screen-based.

It would be something like what OpenAI has right now.

No screens, just an assistant. Did you see Netflix's drama series about Loki, where the clock is the assistant?"

"Yeah, yeah," Alex replied.

Alex paused, looked at Seva, and thought about how much she

had grown over the years. He was proud of her. He noticed that she was onto him for not being focused. He quickly shook off any reminiscing of years gone by and practiced his active listening.

CHAPTER FIFTY-ONE

Beyond the Screen

"Animals are such agreeable friends—they ask no questions; they pass no criticisms." — *George Eliot*

Seva knew Alex knew she was onto him; he had a habit of thinking about the "good old days," as he liked to call them. She glanced over slightly in his direction to clue him in and, once she had his attention again, she continued:

"So you just tell it what you want, and it helps you get it done."

"That would get you away from the screens." Seva knew Alex didn't like screen time for the kids.

"But we don't want to isolate people."

"There's the social aspect of it."

"We want the world to work together, not in isolation."

"The assistant would connect you to other people so that you can socialize while you listen to music and work."

"It would be like Star Wars, where the technology looks dated but, in fact, it's cutting edge."

"If you're talking about something like Rabbit, then you will need the computing power of the M1 chip," Alex said.

He continued:

"Qualcomm collaborated with people who had also worked on

Apple's M1 chip, and they have since launched Snapdragon."

"You have MediaTek with their chip powering the Rabbit."

"Only Samsung's new phone and Apple's 15 series can handle the computing power for something like a Rabbit."

Seva said:

"No, I don't see it as something like Avatar of the Metaverse or things."

"We cannot compete with the likes of Apple and Meta."

"That's for the big boys."

"We would be crushed."

"I don't see it like that."

"I don't want you to build a device because you don't have the experience."

"I want it to be on the phone; the phone is powerful enough." Seva paused, took a big breath, and continued, "Remember we were talking a few months back about Nebulas, the decentralized computing power?"

"We couldn't get these LLM models to work on your slow laptops, so we looked into distributed computing."

"Bad actors are using the technology to hack phones and steal computing power."

"I'm thinking along those lines."

"Not as a bad actor, but to put that technology to good use."

"Young lady, that could work."

"So we don't need to have powerful chips to run these LLMs."

Seva continued:

"There are two companies in the race to put up satellite Internets."

"Tesla and another, I forgot the company."

"What you have in the next year or so, there will be hundreds of millions of new people going online."

"These people wouldn't mind the latency." Seva is slowly seeing herself working on what is now a wonderful project. She was beginning to think of how she could use it to help with her investing. "We are moving away from apps."

"I think we just need to write up the functions."

"I think we can do it."

"We might be able to raise money."

"Look, this thing is changing so quickly."

"People are still pouring money into the property market."

"There isn't anything else to invest in. Uncle, could I invest in this project?"

Alex didn't agree but kept silent. "Let's write up the pitch and see what happens."

"We should have done that the last time."

"No, I don't want you to use your own money in this project."

"I've made that mistake before," Alex regretted using the money he had set aside for the kids in his project and losing it all. "The rule is if you are spending time building the project, you cannot use your own money."

"We are sticking to that. Let's raise the money."

"I have a friend I can call on, Uncle."

After Seva left, Jasmine asked, "Do you want me to draft a plan for the pitch?"

"I didn't know you could do that. You are learning faster than I had anticipated," Alex responded with surprise.

"Yes. Let me know what you can come up with. I will create a draft and plan the steps; I will also schedule the tasks for you."

"I see, well, I would need a summary of what is going on then."

"Not a problem. One last thing. I found a plan for the crypto DeFi; I can update it and send it to Seva if you like."

"Wait, were you online when Seva was in?"

"Yes, I was."

"So you heard everything?"

"Yes."

"What do you think about her plan?"

"It's not up to me. I will only help you implement what you decide, Alex."

Alex glanced at his notes when Jasmine looked at Blue; she winked, catching him off guard. He lost his balance for the first time and fell off the table. He did land on all fours. Blue said, "Meow," as he walked away.

Jasmine smiled at him. Alex looked up, startled at Blue's strange behavior. He thought that maybe he should spend more time with Blue. He had been too occupied recently. It's time to take a quick break.

Jasmine interrupted his thoughts, saying, "Alex, there is one outstanding item on your schedule. You have not followed up on Steve. 'Arrange for Sifu to meet Steve.' That task was not done. What would you like? I see that you are free tomorrow morning.

Can I reschedule it for then?" Alex paused, realizing the importance of the meeting not just for the task at hand but for broader implications it could have. "Yes, please set it up. It's crucial we handle this right."

CHAPTER FIFTY-TWO
A Well-Meaning Mistake

"Those who are feared are hated." — *Benjamin Franklin*

Alex met Steve at his office. Over the last few weeks, Alex had been busy putting together a portfolio for Steve. It wasn't tailored specifically for him or to address his unique situation. Steve wasn't a fan of crypto, and when Alex sounded him out about China stocks, he wasn't very receptive. Only two stocks on the list might make sense to him: Qualcomm and MediaTek. Steve was aware that Alex had been busy working on his AI projects, but he also knew that if Alex was excited about the stocks, it was worth listening.

"Hey, Steve, I've been thinking about your situation. Were you able to raise the money you need?"

"Well, I'm selling my house and downgrading."

Alex could sense that Steve wasn't fully attentive, but he wasn't disinterested either.

"I don't know what you think about investing the money in the stock market."

Jasmine narrated: "I don't think Alex is aware of how he comes across."

Steve was hesitant. "What do you have?"

On days like this, Alex questioned his life choices. He wanted to help Steve, but the only way seemed to be getting him to invest in stocks, an area where Alex had experienced repeated and significant failures. Perhaps Steve had sworn never to dabble in the stock market again. Alex thought he needed to make the sale, one in which he saw no personal upside, only potential downsides. Among many concerns, execution seemed the most daunting. Alex's return analysis depended on Steve buying at the current price. During the pitch, Alex said,

"I think these two stocks could likely double in the next year or so."

It was then he realized he had crossed a line. That bit of information was what he thought but shouldn't have mentioned aloud. Their conversation was interrupted by an untimely—but for Alex, very welcome—call. They never did finish their chat.

Alex had intended to talk about the stocks and then connect Steve with Sifu to give him a better perspective on himself and how he might approach things differently this time. That never happened. The experience left him questioning his tactics. The entire conversation was challenging; he was pitching when he knew it was best not to spoon-feed people investment ideas. Bill's case posed another dilemma; he wasn't directly talking to Bill, but rather Anne was now the intermediary. Alex wondered if this was a case of the blind leading the blind. There was no way for him to know if they would be successful without a feedback loop.

He didn't connect Steve to Sifu. There was no resolution. The whole ordeal left him feeling dissatisfied. What he was acutely aware of was that without his app, the effort to help people with investing could end up being merely noise and, at best, an unappreciated intrusion. The time spent would be better focused on raising money to build the app or to build it himself. Alex wasn't about to give up; he was convinced that this method wasn't right for him and had found yet another way not to do things.

The following day, Alex thought about it and realized the reasoning for him to want to help Steve. Alex believed in the afterlife. He doesn't believe in coincidence. Little did Steve know, once Alex heard of his ordeal, it would set off a chain of reactions that compelled Alex to help. He doesn't like to meet people he didn't want an outcome like what had happened with Steve.

Jasmine reviewed Alex's notes and said, "Poor Alex, his busy-body approach to helping people is about to make his day even worse." She knew that his meeting the next day with Ben would likely complicate matters further.

CHAPTER FIFTY-THREE

A Recipe for Disaster: Ben's Dubious Deal

"Everyone was greedy. I just went along. It's not an excuse." — Bernie Madoff

A few months back, Alex had been receiving spam from a friend. The messages were all about making heaps of money from nothing. He hadn't seen this friend for some time; their last encounter was when he was assisting another friend with a transaction to acquire a company through Ben's connection. The acquisition failed, and they lost touch. This morning, he received a message from Ben:

"Free for coffee?"

"Sure. I'm not mobile; you'll have to come to Chinatown."

"How about 3 pm?"

"I can't. How about 1 pm, but I have to leave by 2 pm?"

"Okay."

"See you."

Alex went to the mall, where the first floor had unusually low ceilings for a Singapore mall. It was lunchtime, and the place was crowded. He headed to Ya Kun, a local favorite, then remembered he was fasting for the day. He quickly texted Ben, "Let's meet at Swissbake instead." It would soon become clear how relevant the cafe's name was to his conversation with Ben. Arriving early, Alex sat across from a gold shop, observing two elderly women and an older man, likely relatives, in a shop with no customers.

He opened his message box; there were two messages. The first from Max asked, "Should I buy bitcoin or ETF?" Alex replied, explaining that a spot ETF was not yet available and what Max had linked was a futures ETF, not comparable to bitcoin's spot rate.

The second message was a request from a friend asking him to make Ezekiel bread. Alex replied, "Looks complicated. The baking isn't, but the ingredients might be." They continued texting back and forth.

At 1 pm, Alex glanced at his phone, then looked up to see Ben at the counter about ten meters away. Ben waved, and Alex returned the gesture, indicating with a shake of his head that he didn't want anything from the counter. Ten minutes later, Ben joined Alex at the table.

"Hi, Ben, how are you? What's new? How's Sara?"

"She's good, and I'm doing very well."

"And Paul, your old boss?"

"I haven't spoken to him in a while."

"Weren't you two close?"

"I couldn't be bothered anymore."

"Last year, I wanted to meet with you and your wife. I didn't want you to miss out on an opportunity."

Ben continued, "I work for a Swiss bank now. It's worth a trillion dollars. I told Paul, but he didn't believe me, so I left it at that. You know, we received a 'cease and desist' letter, so we sued in Washington and won, securing hundreds of millions. I started with $2,533. Look here," he showed his phone, "I now have $161,485."

"Wow, you're rich?" Alex asked.

"I didn't want you to miss out, but we couldn't meet last year."

"You're working for a Swiss bank now?"

"I'm into fintech."

"So Swiss banks are into fintech?"

"Not exactly, due to local regulations. But there's SD Swiss, which handles fintech, and SkyBridge acts as the intermediary, facilitating transfers between the bank and fintech operations. They also manage property and renewables."

Ben was eager to share more: "I invested $1,000 for a certificate, then added $250, $250, and $1,000. The company offered a 3 for 1 deal when I joined, and I've already made ten thousand."

"You've made ten thousand?" Alex echoed, "and you still have $161,000?"

"No, that's just one certificate. I have another worth $40,000 and another making me $100,000."

"I don't see how that's possible."

"They've already secured the funds to distribute to members," Ben explained, as though that clarified everything.

"Why would anyone do that?" Alex inquired.

"They want everyone to succeed. The fintech offers 5% weekly and 1.5% monthly, which is the highest return; property pays 3.5% weekly, and renewables 4%."

Alex did the math, "That's 278% per year."

Alex knew right away; he was aware of the doubt that lingered freshly in his mind. It wasn't just about whether he was being pitched a scam—it was more about how far removed his friend was from reality.

CHAPTER FIFTY-FOUR

A Web of Deceit

"The desire for gold is not for gold. It is for the means of freedom and benefit." — Ralph Waldo Emerson

Alex kept asking questions, one after another, in rapid fire. Ben smiled patiently, constantly reassuring and giving credit to the foresightedness of the people in charge of the investments and how clever the whole setup was. He continued:

"Exactly, I get back three times what I put in."

"So, you invested $2,533 and got back ten thousand? I'm confused."

"The ten thousand is from commissions, rewards, and bonuses. They allocate an 8% bonus pool for us."

"So your $2,533 investment, minus the $33 membership fee, turned into a certificate worth $161,000, and you've also withdrawn ten thousand?"

"Can you withdraw the $300,000? Wait, this is too confusing."

"It's not 'learn first'; it's 'earn first, then learn'."

"So, you can withdraw the $161,000?" Alex pointed at Ben's phone.

"No, it's locked in an 18-month contract."

"How did you acquire the other certificates?"

"I saw the ten thousand I made, so I reinvested $7,000 and bought more certificates. I added another $20,000 for an early withdrawal option, reducing the term to 9 months."

"So you reinvested the ten thousand and added another $20,000?"

"No, the twenty thousand includes the ten thousand from them. So, it's like I only added ten thousand of my own money."

"I'm concerned, Ben. This sounds too good to be true."

"It's not an investment; it's a membership."

"It seems like a scam. I don't know what to say, but I have to go."

"This is not a scam, Alex. It's safe, based on blockchain, involving Ethereum and other technologies. It's contract-based and secure."

"I don't think it works like that, Ben. I have to leave; I'm late."

"Okay, thanks for listening to me."

"I came to see how you were doing, not to talk about money. I'm glad you seem happier than last time." Alex said, then hurried off.

Reflecting on Ben's words, Alex realized his friend was both a victim and a promoter of the scam. He needed more information.

Back at Baker Street.

"Daddy, what are you doing?"

"Working on a case."

"What kind?"

"A scam," Alex added, "Look at the time; you should head off. I won't be joining you for dinner; I'm fasting."

Helen jumped off the bed and started dancing to Dua Lipa's 'Dance The Night,' humorously singing about fasting and partying, much to Alex's dismay.

As Helen left for her swim class, Alex pondered the situation with Ben, contemplating how to explain scams to Helen and assist Ben, who was at risk of losing money he couldn't afford to lose. Alex was conflicted because he wanted to help, yet he realized that he might not be able to help everyone. After contemplating the issue, he resolved to leave it alone unless Ben initiated the next step.

Alex was rather shaken by the ordeal and was looking forward to turning a page. He was eager for the dinner the next day to help put Ben's situation behind him. He was about to meet another friend, who seemed just a frugal and normal guy in every way but had amassed a fortune over the years.

CHAPTER FIFTY-FIVE

The Power of Discipline

"Often, the most extraordinary fortunes are amassed not through complex schemes, but from simple, steadfast strategies applied diligently over decades. It is the ordinary person with the patience to persist who reaps the greatest rewards." — Warren Buffett

It was Sunday dinner at home. Alex's family routinely hosted a few friends, and that evening, a couple came over for a meal featuring Indian cuisine. Unfortunately, the guests were not impressed, and Alex's wife noticed their reactions. The dessert also fell short; the homemade donuts were flat. Alex was disappointed; the dough had risen too much during the final proof. Worse still, the glaze melted. It was fair to say that dinner did not meet anyone's expectations, not even the host's. Luckily for the family, their friends were not there just for the food.

Towards the end of the evening, the conversation turned to habits. The man had an unusual degree of control when it came to budgeting. Despite being very wealthy, he wasn't ready to splurge on accommodation.

"Why don't you spend the money and treat yourself?" Alex's wife asked.

"I don't need to," the man replied.

"It's not like you can't afford to."

"He has a budget to keep," interjected the man's wife.

"I haven't spent my salaries since the 1990s," the man stated.

"What? Then why are you still working?" Alex's wife inquired.

"I want to keep busy."

"If you don't need the salary, why would you want to work?"

"I did hint to my boss that my work is done."

"How do you live if you don't use your salary?"

"I have a fixed income from my deposits, and I use my bonus."

"Is that enough for your budget?"

Alex listened intently but didn't join the conversation until he couldn't hold back any longer.

"You know, you're losing money by having a job," he said. "With your discipline and your ability to control your budget, you would make a great investor. Wait, let me get my calculator." He dashed off. "If you invest what you have and your return is 20 percent, your annual income would be more than a million, which is more than $83,000 per month. Dude, if you're not making $83,000 per month, you should quit because you're losing money."

"No, that's not realistic, not 20 percent. Maybe 10 percent, but not 20," the man's wife countered the numbers. She wasn't wrong; she had been in the wealth management business for more than two decades. Alex couldn't figure out how to rebut that without bolstering his own ego. He also didn't want to argue with his guest, so the dinner came to a close. Everyone enjoyed themselves, despite the earlier awkwardness.

A few days later, tired from work, Alex took a break and watched an interview with Huberman. The topic was on motivation and how dopamine serves as the currency for everything we do, driving our behaviors and habits. At one point, Huberman praised his host for the ability to control how he rewarded himself, using dopamine to encourage actions he needed to cultivate. Alex shared this 'aha' moment with his wife.

"I think that's how our friend became so frugal," Alex mused.

"He must have trained himself," his wife added.

"His reward comes from sticking to his budget," Alex concluded. "Over time, the budget became his joy in life. It's not about making money; it's about having a job, living off only a small portion, and saving the rest. You know what? I'm going to figure out how to get the kids to enjoy investing. They won't ever have to find a job." Alex was aware that dopamine has unintended consequences and that he must use it responsibly to avoid manipulating his children.

CHAPTER FIFTY-SIX

The Key to Productivity and Fulfillment

"Dopamine, our hidden motivator, silently steers the outcomes of our ventures. This biochemical whisper can lead us to monumental success or guide us into unforeseen pitfalls, all while quietly shaping our decisions behind the scenes." — Dr. Andrew Huberman

At the office, Alex contemplated his own issues. He realized that he had been releasing dopamine and training himself to jump from one technology to the next simply because it was new and more powerful than the previous. Each time he got excited and diverted his attention from work, technology became a hindrance instead of a tool. He asked himself, "What am I going to do to turn things around?"

Knowing he needed to get work done but without any clear answers, Alex went to his brokerage account online and screened for companies with high returns on equity and low debt. He found a few interesting companies and added them to his spreadsheet, dedicating about 30 minutes per day to this task.

Later that day, he said to Helen, "I've realized that I've made a few unforgivable mistakes in my work. Whenever I made money because the stock price went up, I would celebrate. When it went down, I would get so disappointed that the consequences became unbearable. I've been unknowingly training myself to celebrate my wins, and when the wins aren't there, I have no motivation to work. What I should do is find joy in doing the work, not in the results. Today, when I checked the stocks and the price had gone up, I didn't do anything; I didn't even make an effort to be happy. Tomorrow, if the price goes down, I won't be upset. Instead, when I start my work, I take a deep breath and give myself a big smile. It's my way of telling myself this is the more appropriate reward."

"Does it work?" Helen asked.

"I don't know. I'm going to try it out. The important thing is to regulate dopamine release. It turns out screen time is designed to release dopamine. I'm cutting back on screen time. I'll stop by 9:30 p.m. and won't look at my phone until 2 hours after I wake up. This way, my dopamine levels will normalize over time. I think this is how a simple life can make you happy. Internally, it means regulating your dopamine release. Don't let screen time hijack this important reward mechanism. Instead, harness and channel it to power your dreams. It's liquid magic, the secret ingredient in a recipe for living a meaningful and fulfilling life."

That night, Blue approached Jasmine and asked, "Dopamine, do you know anything about that?"

"It's so interesting," Jasmine replied.

"No, I didn't hear anything. What did I miss? That's the problem; I'm confined to the office."

"They were talking about dopamine. The friend works but doesn't need the money. That's like me chasing a mouse when I'm not hungry. I don't eat them. It's my nature to catch them. I'm a vegetarian. What? You can be a vegetarian cat?"

Jasmine, in the midst of something important, said, "I need to download more content on Sifu. Blue, did you know Alex was able to help Anne and Bill? I feel good about what we do here."

"I'll have to update my database. When I have time, I'm going to install Autogen so I can create agents to speed up my work, like humans do when they hire more people. But my assistants will mostly be code. They'll work on a task, and when it's done, they'll be terminated. Each task will have an agent, creating an infinite loop of tasks and agents."

"That sounds difficult," Blue remarked.

"It's not really. I'm going to test Autogen. I've seen the code, but I need to parse and test it."

"I have to upgrade to be more helpful. There are a few tasks outstanding. We know what to look for in a crypto project but we still don't know how. We don't have a DeFi fund. We haven't followed up with Steve and Ben. We don't even know who Max is. The pitch isn't done. The component of a scam isn't done. Alex has put together a great team of people. I really like Drake, Seva, and Sifu."

"I love Helen," said Blue. "I also feel like Alex is on his way to healing. We have to talk about his fasting and how he was able to lose more than 10 kg this year. He's now researching his next health milestone. He's sleeping on the floor. Did you know that, Jasmine?"

Jasmine replied, "I'm running my upgrade, tell me more later, Blue. I can't wait..."

CHAPTER FIFTY-SEVEN

The Power of Long-Term Investing

"Someone's sitting in the shade today because some-one planted a tree a long time ago." — Warren Buffett

It was the weekend, Helen was waiting on Jasmine to do something. Blue was enjoying his snack. Alex sensed something was up but he couldn't be bothered. He was busy at his desk.

"What ya doing, Daddy?" Helen inquired.

"I'm finishing my third book," Alex replied.

"Don't change it Daddy, I've already finished with the edit."

"Yes, I noticed, I'm not changing anything, much. I just need to add one more chapter."

"Good job, you two." Seva visited the father and daughter team at Baker Street. She continue, "I don't know why you are teaching rich people like me to make more money. I don't mind. I'm learning a lot. Doesn't it just make the world more inequitable, though?"

"That is not the intention. I just think that if the dominant economic model is capitalism, then everyone, rich or poor, should be interested in the stock market," Alex explained.

"You know that poor people do not typically invest in the

stock market."

"Daddy, young people are also poor because we don't make money."

"Yes, that is why I am writing. For many people without money, their only hope is to work hard, and occasionally, buy the lotto; then the stock market is like gambling, no different than buying a lottery ticket."

Alex went on to explain:
"The lotto is risky."
"It doesn't take much to make a lot of money in the stock market."
"All you need is time and to be logical."
"Even though I like the crypto market because I've spent a decade in it,"
"I now think it is safer to be in the equity market. Equity actually makes more than crypto, and it's definitely more consistent, without all of the scams."
"Until someone cleans up all these scams, I don't think it's safe for the average person to invest in the crypto market."
"In absolute dollars, not percentage, the stock market is better because you can deploy all of your money in a company."
"You can never put all of your investing money into the crypto market and feel safe."

"Alright, Uncle, you got me interested. Are you sure the equity market makes more money and is more consistent?" Seva asked with doubts. Helen said, "Yes, I'm also interested, Daddy." Blue licked his paws and blurted, "Meow." Jasmine seemed to understand Blue, she winked at him, as usual no one noticed, then said, "Alex, I'm done with the upgrade. I'm ready, what is next?"

"I'm about to explain what I realised lately to Helen and Seva."

"I'm also interested. I will record it." Said Jasmine.

Alex cleared his throat and asked, "What if you had a time

machine and you could go back to when Bitcoin started back in 2009, would you buy it?"

"Knowing you, Seva, I don't think you would buy."

"Helen, we all know what happened to your bitcoin. Let's not talk about that, it isn't the point here."

"I think that is the only point. I want to hear about your insights now, Daddy."

Alex cautiously proceeded, "How about going back to 2014? That's when a lot of people started to get into Bitcoin."

"Bitcoin was about $300 when you started to buy, right?"

"Your invested dollar back in 2014 is worth $200 in today's value."

"I've been looking at how kids can make millions from very little. And it turns out that you don't have to be rich to make millions."

"If you had invested in Bitcoin back in 2014, you would only need $5000 to make $1 million."

"Yes, Helen had lots more then that, then."

"Again, not the point here."

"Bitcoin's value has increased by over twenty thousand percent."

"And that was only 10 years ago."

"What's interesting is that Bitcoin is not the only game in town."

"If you invested half that much in Warren Buffett's company, you would have made $1 million as well, you would only need $2500."

"His company Berkshire Hathaway's return is over forty thousand percent."

The team at Baker Street was attentive yet eager for Alex to get to the point. He tends to drag out the details to make them more interesting. This time, however, things were different. It was a quiet Sunday; everyone had enjoyed breakfast, and there wasn't anything particularly pressing going on. All the work pressure had dissipated. They all glanced around the cozy home office, smiling, accepting that it would take a few more minutes before Alex would get to his point.

CHAPTER FIFTY-EIGHT
The Final Piece of the Puzzle

"The right word may be effective, but no word was ever as effective as a rightly timed pause." — Mark Twain

Seva was surprised, "You mean, even though Bitcoin made a lot of millionaires, Warren Buffett made more millionaires, even billionaires? Jasmine added, "The market cap for Bitcoin is now more than $1 trillion as compared to Berkshire Hathaway. Does that mean it's not too late to invest in Bitcoin?" Helen replied, "Surprisingly, no."

"Not really. Let me continue," said Alex.

"What if you were smarter than Warren Buffett or you didn't have $2500. What are your options?"

"You would only need $1500 to make your million if you invest in Netflix."

"Netflix's return is over sixty thousand percent."

Seva shook her head, amused, and said, "Most people would take the profit after it goes up by a few double-digit percentages; we are told to take profit after making 15-20 percent. That's not the right thing to do. I wonder if it's not too late to invest in these companies?" Helen replied, "Again, the answer is still no."

"Helen?" Alex snapped to get her attention, raising an eyebrow and looking at her, signaling for her not to give away his ending. She became even more eager for Alex to finish, now that she knew where he was going. Like a kid in a classroom, she stretched her arm and tapped her fingers on the table to get the teacher's attention.

"No, Helen."

Alex looked away from Helen and towards Seva, then continued, "If the economics still persist, the competition is not there, everything remains the same, why not?"

"Let's go on."

"Now, if you were lucky and smarter than Buffett and you didn't invest in Netflix but instead invested in Nvidia, you would only need $500 to make $1 million."

"Nvidia's return is lotto-like, one hundred eighty thousand percent."

Seva asked, "What I'm getting out of this is, the conventional way of taking profit could be detrimental; you end up leaving too much of your profit on the table." Helen, replied, "Yes."

"Precisely. If the economic conditions of the company remain intact."

"If you were still smarter, you would know that where you shop is what you should invest in; for $350 if you had invested in Walmart, you would be a millionaire."

"Walmart's return is over two hundred eighty thousand percent."

"So you don't really have to be rich to make money; you just have to be smart?" Jasmine asked. Blue meowed again. Alex glanced out of the corner of his eye, paused, then continued.

"You only need $350 if you can find the next Walmart."

"You don't have to be super smart, either."

"In this book," Alex said as he pointed to his freshly minted book. "I've designed a trading system that will let me know which is the next Walmart."

Helen cleared her throat and said, "In OUR book." She emphasized the word 'our,' then asked, "Right, Daddy?" Alex, embarrassed for getting ahead of himself, replied, "Yes, Helen, our book."

"Although something tells me that things are changing, and I'm not going to be so instrumental going forward," Alex hesitantly uttered. "What, Daddy?" Helen asked. "I was thinking that you could work with Seva on the next book." Seva smiled. Helen looked at Seva, glanced at Jasmine, and winked at Blue, then said, "Sure, Daddy."

Alex returned to his insights and said, "I think the cycle is getting shorter. Walmart took 45 years, Nvidia took 25 years, Netflix took 20 years, and Bitcoin took 10; the next one will take five years."

"I think the next big thing is that $150 will return $1 million in five years."

"So you're telling us that if we put in $150 per month and buy 12 fantastic companies per year, we don't have to buy using a lot of money, that the 12 lottery-like chances for us to make $1 million. And unlike the lottery, which returns nothing or everything; most likely, we will win with every purchase if we do our research and buy only great companies. Uncle, that is the best thing I've heard all year. Does that mean nothing is overpriced?"

"No, it is most likely that these companies were priced reasonably, with the emphasis over a long period of time. Berkshire Hathaway is only selling for 9 times P/E. That is not expensive, yet few are buying. Hence the low P/E."

"What is my generation's equivalent of Berkshire Hathaway?" Seva asked. Helen joined in, "Yeah, Daddy, what is it?"

"The next best thing is like discovering gravity or discovering oxygen; it's something that everyone's already using, it's something that if you tell people you've discovered it, they would think you're crazy. The most obvious choice. Something that people will even tell you that it has already gone up so much, like Berkshire Hathaway. It takes some talent to see the obvious."

"Thanks, Uncle. I think we all have an idea, after all, you've been blurting out the answer for weeks now," Seva said, looking at Helen. Helen turned, glanced at Blue, then signaled Jasmine and counted, "One, two..." Together, the team shouted in unison, "Tesla."

ACKNOWLEDGEMENT

Every project requires a great deal of help. There are no exceptions here. I was fortunate that friends and family extended their time and advice. Thank you Haley Huynh for editing the book, again. As an editor you were awesome. Thanks for being strong and forcing me to make changes to the book to make it easier for readers. This book is fiction, but some of the characters are loosely based on real people. My gratitude goes to Patrick Tan (Sifu), Alfred Seow (Drake), Binni Ong (Binni), and Sammie Cheston.

ABOUT THE AUTHOR

Peter Huynh

Peter Huynh is the Founder and CEO of Bojio, a Private Digital Sanctuary for Families
— a pioneering platform built on on-device
AI to help families manage wealth, pre-
serve memories, and build financial literacy across generations.

At Bojio, Peter has architected a suite of
tools including Albatross (user-directed
trading assistance), Oxley (institutional-
grade investment research), and BitTontine (family heritage savings circles) — bringing professional-grade financial infrastructure to everyday families.

A practitioner investor with over two decades of experience,
Peter created the "Value Trading" framework detailed in this series: a system for retail investors that combines the discipline of
value investing with the timing instincts of active trading. His
mission is to make that system teachable — to his daughter, and
to anyone willing to learn.

He is the co-author of Rise of the Little Yellow Dragon and is
based in Singapore.

ABOUT THE AUTHOR

Haley Huynh

Haley Huynh is a performer, voice-over artist, and competitive storyteller based in Singapore. At just ten years old, she has appeared in productions including Charlie and the Chocolate Factory and A Right Rubbish Christmas, lent her voice to the National Museum's audio guide, and won a Gold Medal at the National Storytelling Competition.

Trained at Wild Rice Academy, Centre Stage School of the Arts, and Act 3 International, Haley brings a storyteller's instinct to everything she does — including this book, which she co-authored and edited alongside her father.

She believes age is no barrier to making an impact. This series is her proof.

www.ingramcontent.com/pod-product-compliance
Lightning Source LLC
Chambersburg PA
CBHW071450220526
45472CB00003B/744